A MORE PERFECT UNION

A
MORE
PERFECT
UNION

WHY STRAIGHT AMERICA MUST
STAND UP FOR GAY RIGHTS

RICHARD D. MOHR

BEACON PRESS • BOSTON

BEACON PRESS
25 Beacon Street
Boston, Massachusetts 02108-2892

Beacon Press books
are published under the auspices
of the Unitarian Universalist Association of Congregations.

99 98 97 96 95 94   8 7 6 5 4 3 2 1

Text design by Christine Leonard Raquepaw

Typeset by Technologies 'N Typography

LIBRARY OF CONGRESS CATALOGING-IN-PUBLICATION DATA

Mohr, Richard D.
    A more perfect union : why straight America must stand up for gay
    rights / Richard D. Mohr.
        p. cm.
    ISBN 0-8070-7932-4
    1. Gays—United States. 2. Gays—Civil rights—United States.
I. Title.
HQ76.3.U5M643 1994
305.9′0664—dc20   93-37529

FOR ROBERT W. SWITZER,
whose heartbeat is my peace

CONTENTS

PREFACE

Bicycling together through a midwestern midsummer's night to our village's only gay watering hole, Bob and I are stopped at a red light. A jalopy pulls alongside us in this deserted commercial district. The driver shouts, "Faggots!" He and his partner riding shotgun have all the traits of the classic queerbasher's profile. They are teenaged, bored, white, and male. As a death chill runs my spine, I think "This is it." But then, almost under his breath, the sidekick queries, "Are you motherfuckers gay?" A vertigo of relief doesn't stop a humorous defense from forming. I shape my lips to say, "Just exactly to the extent that we were motherfuckers, we wouldn't be gay, now, would we?" But the light changes—the car lurches, screeches, and rockets into the dark.

Although I have had scarier encounters with toughs, this one is the most haunting. America is at a loss for words when it comes to gays. As I have often recalled that encounter, I wonder what the real question was which lay behind the sidekick's stated one. For surely he wasn't asking for a confirmation of what his friend had had no problem perceiving— that we were in fact gay. I would like to think that the clarity of our love was the giveaway, but my hunch is that it was the leather vests. I now optimistically think that the sidekick in his own stumbling way was asking something like: "What is this gay stuff anyway? Fill me in." Or: "What is the social significance of being gay?" Or: "How am I to act toward you? Here is an opportunity for you to define yourselves to me." If this reading is right, this book is written for him, his parents, his friends, and their relations.

America seems to be at a turning point on gay issues; it is now at least acceptable to inquire about these issues in public discussion. The taboo silencing talk of lesbians and gay men is dissolving. The clearest sign of this shift can be found in the mass media. As little as a decade back the *New York Times* refused even to print the word gay, and it nearly blacked out coverage of gays and AIDS in the first two-thirds of the 1980s; but now it carries more gay news than the national gay news magazine *The Advocate.* The 1987 lesbian and gay March on Washington gleaned no national news coverage for its quarter million marchers. The 1993 March generated national features even before its hundreds of thousands arrived to hear six hours of speeches, which were nationally televised across C-SPAN. The conservative *U.S. News and World Report* carries editorials supporting domestic partner legislation. Smiling lesbian couples beam from the cover of *Newsweek.* And little barriers to talk are falling too. Along with the usual hateful remarks and telephone numbers, truckstop graffiti now includes elaborate commentaries on homophobia and gay life in America. Children can now read a nationally syndicated comic strip with a gay male character. And for the first time New York City's elected community school boards have been joined by open lesbians, who will raise gay issues affecting the education and the moral training of the young.

The lifting of the taboo over speech will have (I predict) a significant effect on the public lives of many nongay people. Studies have shown that, on gay issues, people are greatly affected in their opinions by how they think other people will perceive them. Taboos encourage, indeed enforce, the aping of opinions from one person to the next, causing them to circulate independently of both critical assessment and authentic feeling. The result is that many nongay people feel socially required to be gay-fearing or gay-hating, even when they are not homophobic by personal inclination. Many people do not on their own feel hostile to gays, but feel compelled to go along with the rituals that degrade and silence gay life, lest they themselves be viewed as morally beyond the pale. As the taboos over talking about gay men and lesbians break down, so too will the echoes and apings that have maintained so many of the social forces directed against gays. Nongay people will be able to express in public contexts their own real feelings—which I do not believe to be uniformly anti-gay.

But this new opportunity raises the question, "Now that we can talk, what should we be saying?" Especially for nongay people, the long night of socially enforced silence on gay issues has created a void in social thinking. Nothing could provide a clearer example of this void than the heated, wildly gyrating, but anemic debates which raged through 1993 over how or whether gays should be allowed in the armed forces. Media channels are open, but little of substance is being conveyed. Suddenly gays are on the national playing field, but no one is quite sure what the game is, let alone what the stakes are and what winning and losing might mean.

By both drawing attention to that which is special about gay experience and applying to that experience moral precepts and arguments which Americans as a people have worked through in other areas of national life, this little book hopes to begin filling in this void in our social thinking and public policy toward gays. Taking the old equipment into new territory will not be as hopeless a journey as a trip to the North Pole conducted in summer clothes and guided by maps of the Italian lakes, neither will it be a simple walk around the block. It will be an adventure, perhaps one of personal discovery and transformation.

The book addresses a wide spectrum of human behaviors and relations. The book's content moves across the human spectrum from the intimate to the impersonal, the individual to the social, the private to the political. After a ground-clearing introductory chapter addressing prejudice against and stereotypes surrounding gays comes a chapter which looks at intimacy, in particular at the proper relationships between sex, love, and privacy. The next chapter explores the meaning of marriage and gays' access to it.

The following chapters address the gay person as a social creature and community member. They explore civil relations, relations conducted between people at arm's length. They ask how people can be fair to each other in the workaday activities of the public sphere. Chapter 4 explores what the elusive notion of social equality really means in America and how America understands what a minority is in a moral sense. Chapter 5 considers whether standard civil rights protections in employment, housing, and public services should be extended to gays. Chapter 6 asks, in the face of a re-ghettoization of the AIDS crisis and renewed efforts to use coercion to solve the crisis, what the government should and should not be doing about AIDS. Finally, chapter 7 addresses gay issues at the point where the individual becomes impersonally fused with the functions of state—becomes the citizen-soldier. In some closing remarks, I suggest a variety of ways in which ordinary citizens can help put the book's ideals into practice.

Soon after our bicycling encounter, Bob and I held a large party in our small home to celebrate our first ten years together. The event held out prospects for reenactments of *When Worlds Collide,* for we had invited people from all the diverse walks of our lives—academics and not, gays and not, wealthy and unemployed, young and old, farmers and townfolk. Most of our guests would know only a few people among the others. On arriving, they were instructed to introduce themselves to at least three people they had never seen before. Most did and all worked out fine. Gays and nongays, though, responded quite differently to the party as a social ritual—a dimension of the event to which Bob and I had not given much thought in advance. Judging from the unexpected bestowal of presents, I took it that the nongay folk were treating the event roughly on a par with a fiftieth wedding anniversary. Given the extreme compression of time in the gay world—generations seem to pass in, say, six years rather than the usual twenty-five—this appraisal is on some calibrations perhaps not too far off the mark. Surprising to me was that gays seemed to take the event far less seriously than the nongays. This difference may have been the work of lurking self-hatred on the part of gays, a reluctance to acknowledge our right to celebrate a marriage anniversary. Or it may have been instead that nongays have so many traditions to fall back on, they can almost automatically address any oddness that pops up when old ways are translated onto new turf. In any case, the party made me cautiously optimistic that gays and nongays can move together toward justice even in the areas of social policy which seem to be most troubling to mainstream culture. My hope is that this book will help in that convergence.

August 1993
Urbana, Illinois

CHAPTER 1

Prejudice and Homosexuality

Who are gays anyway? Though the number of gays in America is hotly disputed, studies agree that gays are distributed through every stripe and stratum of Americans. Who are homosexuals? They are your friends, your minister, your teacher, your bankteller, your doctor, your mailcarrier, your officemate, your roommate, your congressional representative, your sibling, parent, and spouse. They are we. We are everywhere, virtually all ordinary, virtually all unknown.

Ignorance about gays, however, has not stopped people's minds from being filled with stereotypes about gays. Society holds two oddly contradictory groups of anti-gay stereotypes. One revolves around an individual's allegedly confused gender identity: lesbians are females who want to be, or at least look and act like, men—bulldykes, diesel dykes; while gay men are males who want to be, or at least look and act like, women—queens, fairies, nances, limp-wrists, nellies, sissies, aunties. These stereotypes of mismatches between biological sex and socially defined gender provide the materials through which lesbians and gay men become the butts of ethniclike jokes. These stereotypes and jokes, though derisive, basically view lesbians and gay men as ridiculous. For example: "How many fags does it take to change a light bulb?" Answer: "Eight—one to replace it and seven to scream 'Faaaaaabulous!'"

The other set of stereotypes revolves around gays as a pervasive sinister conspiratorial threat. The core stereotype here is that of the gay person—especially gay man—as child molester, and more generally as sex-crazed maniac. Homosexuality here is viewed as a vampirelike corruptive contagion. These stereotypes carry with them fears of the very destruction of family and civilization itself. Now, that which is essentially ridiculous can hardly have such a staggering effect. Something must be afoot.

Clarifying the nature of stereotypes can help make sense of this incoherent amalgam. Stereotypes are not simply false generalizations from a skewed sample of cases examined. Admittedly, false generalizing plays some part in the stereotypes society holds about gays and other groups. If, for instance, one takes as one's sample gay men who are in psychiatric hospitals or prisons, as was done in nearly all early investigations, not surprisingly one will probably find them to be of a crazed or criminal cast. Such false generalizations, though, simply confirm beliefs already held on independent grounds, ones that likely led the investigator to the prison and psychiatric ward to begin with. Evelyn Hooker, who in the late 1950s carried out the first rigorous studies of nonclinical gay men, found that psychiatrists, when presented with case files including all the standard diagnostic psychological profiles—but omitting indications of sexual orientation—were unable to distinguish gay files from nongay ones, even though they believed gay men to be crazy.

These studies proved a profound embarrassment to the psychiatric establishment, which has profited throughout the century by attempting to "cure" allegedly insane gays. The studies led eventually to the decision by the American Psychiatric Association in 1973 to drop homosexuality from its registry of mental illnesses. Nevertheless, the stereotype of gays as "sick" continues to thrive in the mind of America.

False generalizations help maintain stereotypes; they do not form them. As the history of Hooker's discoveries shows, stereotypes have a life beyond facts; their origin lies in a culture's ideology—the general system of beliefs by which it lives—and they are sustained across generations by diverse cultural transmissions, including slang and jokes, which usually don't even purport to have a scientific basis. Stereotypes, then, are not the products of bad science, but reflections of society's conception of itself.

Understanding this much, it is easy to see how stereotypes about gays as gender-confused reinforce still powerful gender roles in American society. What these stereotypes presume about gays and condemn is the notion that freely choosing one's social roles independently of one's biological sex might threaten many guiding social divisions, both domestic and commercial. Blurred would be the socially sex-linked distinctions between breadwinner and homemaker, boss and secretary, doctor and nurse, protector and protected, even God and His world. The accusations "fag" and "dyke" serve in significant part to keep women in their place and to prevent men from breaking ranks and ceding away theirs.

The stereotypes of gays as destroyers of civilization function to displace (possibly irresolvable) social problems from their actual source to a remote and (society hopes) manageable one. For example, the stereotype of the gay person as child molester functions to give the traditionally defined family unit a false sheen of innocence. It keeps the unit from being examined too closely for incest, child abuse, wife-battering, and the terrorizing of women and children by a father's constant threats. The stereotype teaches that the problems of the family are not internal to it, but external.

If this account of stereotypes holds, society has been profoundly immoral. For its treatment of gays is a grand-scale rationalization, a moral sleight-of-hand. The problem is not that society's usual standards of evidence and procedure in decision making have been misapplied to gays, rather when it comes to gays, the standards themselves have simply been ruled out of court and disregarded in favor of mechanisms that encourage unexamined fear and hatred.

Partly because lots of people suppose they don't know any gay people and partly through the maintaining of stereotypes, society at large is unaware of the many ways in which gays are subject to discrimination in consequence of widespread fear and hatred. Contributing to this social ignorance of discrimination is the difficulty for gay people, as an invisible minority, even to complain of discrimination. If one is gay, the act of registering a complaint suddenly targets oneself as a stigmatized person, and so, especially in the absence of any protection against discrimination, simply invites additional discrimination. So, discrimination against gays, like rape, goes seriously underreported. Even so, known discrimination is massive.

Annual studies by the National Gay and Lesbian Task Force have consistently found that over 90 percent of gay men and lesbians have been victims of violence or harassment in some form on the basis of their sexual orientation. Greater than one in five gay men and nearly one in ten lesbians have been punched, hit, or kicked; a quarter of all gays have had objects thrown at them; a third have been chased; a third have been sexually harassed, and 14 percent have been spit on, all just for being perceived to be gay.

The most extreme form of anti-gay violence is queerbashing—where groups of young men target a person who they suppose is a gay man and beat and kick him unconscious and sometimes to death amid a torrent of taunts and slurs. Few such cases with gay victims reach the courts. Those that do are marked by inequitable procedures and results. Frequently judges will describe queerbashers as "just all-American boys." A District of Columbia judge handed suspended sentences to queerbashers whose victim had been stalked, beaten, stripped at knife point, slashed, kicked, threatened with castration, and pissed on, because the judge thought the bashers were good boys at heart—they went to a religious prep school. In 1989, a judge in Dallas handed a sentence he acknowledged as light to the eighteen-year-old murderer of two gay men because the murderer had killed them in a gay cruising zone, where the judge said they might have been molesting children. The judge thereby justified a form of vigilantism that bears a striking resemblance to the lynching of black men on the grounds that they might molest white women. Indeed, queerbashing has the same function that past lynchings of blacks had—to keep a whole stigmatized group in line. As with lynchings, society has routinely averted its eyes, giving its permission or even tacit approval to violence and harassment.

Police and juries often will simply discount testimony from gays; they frequently construe assaults on and murders of gays as "justified" self-defense. The killer simply claims his act was an understandably panicked response to a sexual overture. Alternatively, when guilt seems patent, juries will accept highly implausible "diminished capacity" defenses, as in the case of Dan White's 1978 assassination of openly gay San Francisco city councilman Harvey Milk. Hostess Twinkies made him do it, or so the successful defense went. These inequitable procedures collectively show that the life and liberty of gays, like those of blacks, simply count for less than the life and liberty of members of the dominant culture.

Gays are also subject to widespread discrimination in employment. Governments are leading offenders here. They do a lot of discriminating themselves, require that others do it, and set precedents favoring discrimination in the private sector. First and foremost, the armed forces discriminate against lesbians and gay men. The federal government has also denied gay men and lesbians employment in the CIA, FBI, and the National Security Agency—and continues to defend such discrimination in the courts. The government refuses to give security clearances to gays and so forces the country's considerable private sector military and aerospace contractors to fire employees known to be gay and to avoid hiring those perceived to be gay. State and local governments regularly fire gay teachers, policemen, firemen, social workers, and anyone who has contact with the public. Further, state licensing laws (though frequently honored only in the breach) officially bar gays from a vast array of occupations and professions—everything from doctors, lawyers, accountants, and nurses to hairdressers, morticians, even used-car dealers.

Gays are subject to discrimination in a wide variety of other ways, including private-sector employment, public accommodations, housing, insurance of all types, custody, adoption, and zoning regulations that bar "singles" or "nonrelated" couples from living together. A 1988 study by the Congressional Office of Technology Assessment found that a third of America's insurance companies openly admit that they discriminate against lesbians and gay men. In nearly half the states, same-sex sexual behavior is illegal.

Legal sanctions, discrimination, and the absorption by gays of society's hatred all interact to impede and, for some, block altogether the ability of gay men and lesbians to create and maintain significant personal relations with loved ones. Every facet of life is affected by discrimination. Only the most compelling reasons could possibly justify it.

Many people suppose society's treatment of gays is justified because they think gays are extremely immoral. To evaluate this claim, different senses of "moral" must be distinguished. Sometimes "morality" means the values generally held by members of a society—its mores, norms, and customs. On this understanding, gays certainly are not moral: lots of people hate them, and social customs are designed to register widespread disapproval of gays. The problem here is that this sense of morality is merely a descriptive one. Every society has this kind of morality—even Nazi society, which had racism and mob rule as central features of its "morality" understood in this sense. Before one can use the notion of morality to praise or condemn behavior, what is needed is a sense of morality that is prescriptive or normative.

As the Nazi example makes clear, the fact that a belief or claim is descriptively moral does not entail that it is normatively moral. A lot of people in a society saying that something is good, even over aeons, does not make it so. The rejection of the long history of the socially approved and state-enforced institution of slavery is another good example of this principle at work. Slavery would be wrong even if nearly everyone liked it. So consistency and fairness require that one abandon the belief that gays are immoral simply because most people dislike or disapprove of gays.

Furthermore, recent historical and anthropological research has shown that opinion about gays has been by no means universally negative. It has varied widely even within the larger part of the Christian era and even within the Church itself. There are even current societies—most notably in Papua New Guinea—where compulsory homosexual behavior is integral to the rites of male maturity. Within the last thirty years, American society has undergone a grand turnabout from deeply ingrained, nearly total condemnation to nearly total acceptance on two emotionally charged "moral" or "family" issues—contraception and divorce. Society holds its current descriptive morality of gays not because it has to, but because it chooses to.

Clearly popular opinion and custom are not enough to ground moral condemnation of homosexuality. Religious arguments are also frequently used to condemn homosexuality. Such arguments usually proceed along two lines. One claims that the condemnation is a direct revelation of God, usually through the Bible. The other sees condemnation in God's plan as manifested in nature; homosexuality (it is claimed) is "contrary to nature."

One of the more remarkable discoveries of recent gay research is that the Bible may not be as univocal in its condemnation of homosexuality as many have believed. Christ never mentions homosexuality. Recent interpreters of the Old Testament have pointed out that the story of Lot at Sodom is probably intended to condemn inhospitality rather than homosexuality. Further, some of the Old Testament condemnations of homosexuality seem simply to be ways of tarring those of the Israelites' opponents who happen to accept homosexual practices when the Israelites themselves did not. If so, the condemnation is merely a quirk of history and rhetoric rather than a moral precept.

What does seem clear is that those who regularly cite the Bible to condemn an activity like homosexual sex do so by reading it selectively. Do clergy who cite what they take to be condemnations of homosexuality in Leviticus maintain in their lives all the hygienic, dietary, and marital laws of Leviticus? If they cite the story of Lot at Sodom to condemn homosexuality, do they also cite the story of Lot in the Cave to condone incestuous rape? It seems then not that the Bible is being used to ground condemnations of homosexuality as much as society's dislike of homosexuality is being used to interpret the Bible.

Even if a consistent portrait of condemnation could be gleaned from the Bible, what social significance should it be given? One of the guiding principles of society, enshrined in the Constitution as a check against the government, is that decisions affecting social policy are not made on religious grounds. The Religious Right has been successful in thwarting sodomy law reform, in defunding gay safe-sex literature and gay art, and in blocking the introduction of gay materials into school curriculums. If the real ground of the alleged immorality invoked by governments to discriminate against gays is religious (as it seems to be in these cases), then one of the major commitments of our nation is violated. Religious belief is a fine guide around which a person might organize his own life, but an awful instrument around which to organize someone else's life.

In the second kind of religious argument, people try to justify society's treatment of gays by saying they are unnatural. Though the accusation of unnaturalness looks whimsical, it is usually hurled against homosexuality with venom of forethought. It carries a high emotional charge, usually expressing disgust and evincing queasiness. Probably it is nothing but an emotional charge. For people get equally disgusted and queasy at all sorts of things which are perfectly natural and which could hardly be fit subjects for moral condemnation. Two typical examples in current American culture are some people's responses to mothers breastfeeding in public and to women who do not shave body hair. Similarly people fling the term "unnatural" at gays in the same breath and with the same force as when they call gays "sick" and "gross." When people have strong emotional reactions, as they do in these cases, without being able to give good reasons for them, they can hardly be thought of as operating morally, but more likely as obsessed and manic.

When "nature" is taken in technical rather than ordinary usages, it also cannot ground a charge of homosexual immorality. When unnatural means "by artifice" or "made by humans," it can be pointed out that virtually everything that is good about life is unnatural in this sense. The chief feature that distinguishes people from other animals is people's very ability to make over the world to meet their needs and desires. Indeed people's well-being depends upon these departures from nature. On this understanding of human nature and the natural, homosexuality is perfectly unobjectionable; it is simply a means by which some people adapt nature to fulfill their desires and needs.

Another technical sense of natural is that something is natural and so, good, if it fulfills some function in nature. On this view, homosexuality is unnatural because it violates the function of genitals, which is to make babies. One problem with this view is that lots of bodily parts have lots of functions and just because some one activity can be fulfilled by only one organ (say, the mouth for eating), this activity does not condemn other functions of the organ as immoral (say, the mouth for talking, licking stamps, or blowing bubbles). So the possible use of the genitals to produce children does not, without more, condemn the use of the genitals for other purposes, say, achieving ecstasy and intimacy.

The notion of function seemed like it might ground moral authority, but instead it turns out that moral authority is needed to define "proper function." If God is the moral authority, we are back to square one—holding others accountable to our own religious beliefs.

Finally, people sometimes attempt to establish authority for a moral obligation to use bodily parts in a certain fashion simply by claiming that moral laws are natural laws and vice versa. On this account, inanimate objects and plants are good in that they follow natural laws by necessity, animals follow them by instinct, and persons follow them by a rational will. People are special in that they must first discover the laws that govern them. Now, even if one believes the view—dubious in the post-Newtonian, post-Darwinian world—that natural laws in the usual sense ($e=mc^2$, for instance) have some moral content, it is not at all clear how one is to discover the laws in nature that apply to people.

On the one hand, if one looks to people themselves for a model—and looks hard enough—one finds amazing variety, including homosexual relations as a social ideal (as in upper-class fifth-century Athens) and even as socially mandatory (as in some Melanesian initiation rites today). When one looks to people, one is simply unable to strip away the layers of social custom, history, and taboo in order to see what's really there to any degree more specific than that people are the creatures that make over their world and are capable of abstract thought. That this is so should raise doubts that neutral principles are to be found in human nature that will condemn homosexuality.

On the other hand, if one looks to nature apart from people for models, the possibilities are staggering. There are fish that change sex over their lifetimes: should we "follow nature" and be operative transsexuals? Orangutans, genetically our next of kin, live completely solitary lives without social organization of any kind among adults: ought we to "follow nature" and be hermits? There are many species where only two members per generation reproduce: shall we be bees? The search in nature for people's purpose far from finding sure models for action is likely to leave one morally rudderless.

But (it might also be asked) aren't gays willfully the way they are? It is widely conceded that if sexual orientation is something over which an individual—for whatever reason—has virtually no control, then discrimination against gays is presumptively wrong, as it is against racial and ethnic classes.

Attempts to answer the question whether or not sexual orientation is something that is reasonably thought to be within one's own control usually appeal simply to various claims of the biological or "mental" sciences. But the ensuing debate over genes, hormones, hypothalamuses, twins, early childhood development, and the like is as unnecessary as it is currently inconclusive. All that is needed to answer the question is to look at the actual experience of lesbians and gay men in current society, and it becomes fairly clear that sexual orientation is not likely a matter of choice.

On the one hand, the "choice" of the gender of a sexual partner does not seem to express a trivial desire which might as easily be fulfilled by a simple substitution of the desired object. Picking the gender of a sex partner is decidedly dissimilar, that is, to such activities as picking a flavor of ice cream. If an ice cream parlor is out of one's flavor, one simply picks another. And if people were persecuted, threatened with jail terms, shattered careers, loss of family and housing, and the like for eating, say, Rocky Road ice cream, no one would ever eat it. Everyone would pick another easily available flavor. That gay people abide in being gay even in the face of persecution suggests that being gay is not a matter of easy choice.

On the other hand, even if establishing a sexual orientation is not like making a relatively trivial choice, perhaps it is like

making the central and serious life choices by which individuals try to establish themselves as being of some type or
having some occupation. Again, if one examines gay experience, this seems not to be the general case. For one virtually
never sees anyone setting out to become a homosexual, in
the way one does see people setting out to become doctors,
lawyers, and bricklayers. One does not find gays-to-be picking some end—"At some point in the future, I want to
become a homosexual"—and then setting about planning
and acquiring the ways and means to that end, in the way
one does see people deciding that they want to become
lawyers, and then sees them plan what courses to take and
what sort of temperaments, habits, and skills to develop in
order to become lawyers. Typically, gays-to-be simply find
themselves having homosexual encounters and yet, at least
initially, resisting quite strongly the identification of being
homosexual. Such a person even very likely resists having
such encounters, but ends up having them anyway. Only with
time, luck, and great personal effort, but sometimes never,
does the person gradually come to accept her or his orientation, to view it as a given material condition of life, coming
as all materials do with certain capacities and limitations. The
person begins to act in accordance with his or her orientation
and its capacities, seeing its actualization as a requisite for an
integrated personality and as a central component of personal well-being. As a result, the experience of coming out
to oneself has for gays the basic structure of a discovery, not
the structure of a choice. And far from signaling immorality,
coming out to others affords one of the few remaining opportunities in ever more bureaucratic, technological, and so-
cialistic societies to manifest courage.

How would society at large be changed if gays were socially accepted? Suggestions to change social policy with regard to gays are invariably met with claims that to do so would invite the destruction of civilization itself: after all isn't that what did Rome in? Actually, Rome's decay paralleled not the flourishing of homosexuality but its repression under the later Christianized emperors. Predictions of American civilization's imminent demise have been as premature as they have been frequent. Civilization has shown itself to be rather resilient here, in large part because of the country's traditional commitments to respect for privacy, to individual liberties, and especially to people minding their own business. These all give society an open texture and the flexibility to try out things to see what works. And because of this, one now need not speculate about what changes reforms in gay social policy might bring to society at large. For many reforms have already been tried.

Half the states have decriminalized lesbian and gay male sex acts. Can you guess which of the following states still have sodomy laws: Wisconsin, Minnesota; New Mexico, Arizona; Vermont, New Hampshire; Nebraska, Kansas? One from each pair does and one does not have sodomy laws. And yet one would be hard pressed to point out any substantial social differences between the members of each pair. (If you're interested: the second of each pair still has them.) Empirical studies have shown that there is no increase in other crimes in states that have decriminalized homosexual sex acts.

Neither has the passage of legislation barring discrimination against gays ushered in the end of civilization. Nearly a hundred counties and municipalities, including some of the country's largest cities (like Chicago and New York City), have passed such statutes, as have eight states: Wisconsin, Connecticut, Massachusetts, Hawaii, New Jersey, Vermont, California, and Minnesota. Again, no more brimstone has fallen on these places than elsewhere. Staunchly anti-gay cities, like Miami and Houston, have not been spared the AIDS crisis.

Berkeley, California, followed by a couple dozen other cities including New York, has even passed "domestic partner" legislation giving gay couples at least some of the same rights to city benefits as are held by heterosexually married couples, and yet Berkeley has not become more weird than it already was. A number of major universities (including Harvard, Stanford, and the University of Chicago) and respected corporations (including Levi Strauss and Company, the Montefiore Medical Center of New York, and Apple Computer, Inc.) have also been following Berkeley's lead. Lesbian and gay marriages are legal in Denmark (as of 1989) and in Norway (1993). In May of 1993, Hawaii's Supreme Court ruled that the state's law requiring spouses to be of different genders is a violation of the state's Equal Rights Amendment and can be upheld in further litigation only if the law's discrimination against same-sex couples (implausibly) can be shown to be necessary to a compelling state interest.

Seemingly hysterical predictions that the American family would collapse if such reforms passed have proven false, just as the same dire predictions that the availability of divorce would lessen the ideal and desirability of marriage proved unfounded. Indeed if current discrimination, which drives gays into hiding and into anonymous relations, ended, far from seeing gays destroying American families, one would see gays forming them.

If discrimination ceased, gay men and lesbians would enter the mainstream of the human community openly and with self-respect. The energies that the typical gay person wastes in the anxiety of leading a day-to-day existence of systematic disguise would be released for use in personal flourishing. From this release would be generated the many benefits that accrue to a society when its individual members thrive.

Society would be richer for acknowledging another aspect of human diversity. Families with gay members would develop relations based on truth and trust rather than lies and fear. And the heterosexual majority would be better off for knowing that they are no longer trampling their gay friends and neighbors.

Finally and perhaps paradoxically, in extending to gays the rights and benefits it has reserved for its dominant culture, America would confirm its deeply held vision of itself as a morally progressing nation, a nation itself advancing and serving as a beacon for others—especially with regard to human rights. The words with which our national pledge ends—"with liberty and justice for all"—are not a description of the present, but a call for the future. America is a nation given to a prophetic political rhetoric which acknowledges that morality is not arbitrary and that justice is not merely the expression of the current collective will. It is this vision that led the black civil rights movement to its successes. Those senators and representatives who opposed that movement and its centerpiece, the 1964 Civil Rights Act, on obscurantist grounds, but who lived long enough and were noble enough, came in time to express their heartfelt regret and shame at what they had done. It is to be hoped and someday to be expected that those who now grasp at anything to oppose the extension of that which is best about America to gays will one day feel the same.

CHAPTER 2

Sexual Privacy

██████████ Atlanta. Early morning. August 3, 1982. A knock at the door. A policeman asks for Michael Hardwick. His roommate doesn't know whether he's in, but points the officer down the hall. Through a slit formed by a door-frame out of plumb, the officer peers into Hardwick's room—and continues peering for a minute or two before crashing in to arrest Hardwick for the consensual gay sex he is having in his own bedroom. Hardwick and his companion are handcuffed to the floor of the squad car for half an hour. At headquarters, police and inmates taunt and humiliate Hardwick—"fag, fag, fag"—for twelve hours before his friends are allowed to pay bail. Four years later, in *Bowers v. Hardwick,* the Supreme Court rules that Georgia may jail Hardwick for ten years for his act of lovemaking—that privacy rights do not reach to gay sex.

Even when gay men and lesbians are not arrested for breaking sodomy laws, the laws' existence and acceptance generate devastating spin-off effects. In custody cases, for example, judges are quick to remove children from openly lesbian mothers, claiming that as admitted felons, the mothers are obviously unfit. Similarly, judges consider the admission of regular violations of sodomy laws as a showing of bad moral character, and so justify discrimination against gays as policemen, teachers, and in scores of other jobs that require state licensing. Indeed, federal judges have regularly held that if it is permissible for the state to make gay sex illegal, it must be further constitutionally permissible to discriminate in general against homosexuals. And, sodomy laws are the engines that justify and legally prop up sexual solicitation laws, which *are* regularly enforced, especially against male homosexuals, who frequently, in consequence, lose jobs and families—and sometimes commit suicide.

Nearly half the states still have sodomy laws. In a few of these states (for example, Texas and Tennessee), sodomy laws explicitly discriminate against gays by applying only to same-sex encounters. In the remainder of these states, though their sodomy laws are worded neutrally in that they apply to gays and nongays alike, still given the geography of human bodies and what usually counts as sex, these laws have the effect of merely regulating the sex lives of nongays, while officially denying any sex life at all to gays. The laws' surface neutrality is therefore phony, and gays have a special interest in seeing all sodomy laws eliminated in favor of consenting adult laws. But legislative reform was stalled even before *Bowers,* and state judicial reform has had only one success since *Bowers*— in Kentucky. At that rate of reform, it would take a century and a half before all the remaining states eliminated their sodomy laws. Clearly the issue needs rethinking.

How should we think morally about gays and sex and privacy? It is noteworthy that over a very broad spectrum of political opinion, people agree that there is a general right to privacy. In the broad middle band of the political spectrum, including liberals and conservatives alike and all the currently live political positions in the United States, everyone agrees that there is a right to privacy. But disagreement breaks out over what specific protections this general right encompasses. Liberals view it as entailing such protections as a right to abortion, a right to own pornography, and possibly even a right to own drugs; conservatives view it rather as encompassing such rights as a right to unrestricted use of property, a right to own automatic weapons, and a right to do business with whomever one wants. In this chapter, I assume, along with the rest of the nation, that there is a right to privacy. What I will argue is that a right to have consensual sex, including gay sex, falls under this right to privacy. I will give three moral arguments which explain why consensual sex between adults engages various dimensions of privacy in ways that invoke privacy as a right.

The breadth of agreement over the existence of a right to privacy is (I believe) a tacit acknowledgment that privacy rights in part derive from the very nature of human agency, more particularly from the fact that, unlike angels, we have bodies, indeed in some sense *are* our bodies. The distinctive relation that a person holds to his or her own body grounds an important dimension of sexual privacy and of privacy more generally. What one does to one's body or has done to one's own body has a special status underwritten by the importance of the body itself.

The body is the foundation for a person's being in the world at all, for his projection of himself into the world through actions, and for his instilling value in things. The body is not merely necessary for existence and action—as food, shelter, and a kidney machine might be—but also is part of that *in virtue of which* a person is and acts. If a person is to be free in any of her actions, she must therefore have control of her own body—not in the sense of doing *with* it as she will, but doing *to* it as she will—so that it is hers. In order that an action is one's own, it is not enough that the action be the product of one's intentions. For one's intentions are presented not merely by and through but inextricably *with* one's body. Therefore, if one's acts are to be one's own, one's body as well as one's intentions must be one's own.

Now, no one could assert that one's thoughts and intentions were really one's own—formed the basis of a free action—if they were the thoughts one just happened to have, if, for instance, they were simply installed there in one's mind by brainwashing, electrodes, or God. And they would not even be one's own if one fell into them by chance—if they just happened to be "in the air" and one passively absorbed them. The ideas would be one's own in a significant sense only if one had considered them, worked them over, appropriated them, and especially if one produced them new. Without the last, at least as a possibility, one's thoughts are not truly one's own.

Similarly, if one's existence is to be one's own other than by accident and if one's actions are to be free, one's body must not belong to one merely by accident. One must not be forced merely to accept what is given by nature or by others' volitions. One must be permitted the opportunity to mold it, shape it, alter it, and even to make it as boldly new as it is capable, not as others allow, assuming, of course, all the usual constraints on what one may do *to* others *with* it. One may not reshape one's fist by breaking it on another's skull. One may not be permitted to cut one's hand at all if that would cause one preemptively to fail of some duty justifiably incumbent upon one—say, military service in defensive war. But such relatively clear exceptions aside, one must be free to do to one's body as one sees fit, if one is to be free at all.

Another route to the same conclusion is to notice that a person's body is not just one more damn thing in the world that she might have or own, but rather has a special value and standing as that in virtue of which she possesses other things and as the chief means by which other things come to have value. "My body" has a wholly different status than even "my house." A house belongs to its owner because he built it with his body, or bought it with fruits of the labor his body provided him. An unappropriated object in the world becomes one's own as one mixes one's labor with it, for it would then be unjust for anyone else to take it. No one else in this circumstance deserves it.

One's property rights then devolve from a special status that one has as a body. If some of the world is one's own, it is so because of one's body. The body is not merely a necessary condition for one's appropriating what is one's own, it is also the chief causal condition for appropriation. If one speaks of one's body as "mine," it is nevertheless not subject to the same restraints and controls as other things that one owns, for it is morally and causally prior to their being one's own.

A person's body is therefore not available to government for its legitimate projects in the way her (other) property is. Government cannot prevent the individual from valuing herself and possessing herself and yet still suppose that—at least in some areas such as those protected by substantive rights—she is not merely a tool of and for government but has her own projects and values that take precedence. If there are any substantive liberties, a person has a right to instill value in herself and possess herself.

A very powerful right to privacy then is generated by and over the body because of its special status in one's projects, one's values, and one's very presence in the world. As the means by which one both projects oneself into the world and appropriates what is one's own to oneself, the body engenders special protections for one's actions that chiefly affect it, even if the features of the world which it affects, produces or appropriates are not covered by the same right and thus remain generally subject to state control.

The general right to control one's body has at its core a cluster of specific, bodily based liberties: one has a strong presumptive right to feed one's body, to manipulate it, to exercise it, to dress it as one sees fit, to seek medical treatment, to inject foreign bodies into it, to permit others to do so, to touch it, to have others touch it, to allow others to present their bodies to it, and to be the chief governor and guarantor of one's own feelings, emotions, and sensations—compatible with a like ability on the part of others and with other requirements for civil society. Consensual sex between adults engages and nearly exhausts the core protections of the general right to bodily based privacy. Indeed it comes close to being a perfect or complete exemplification of its provisions.

Only when one's control of one's body is protected, does one have a right to bodily integrity, and only when one has bodily integrity is one a person at all. Any moral systems, then, in which persons are a locus of value will be obliged to protect from government those persons' acts of consensual sex.

The specific sort of "doings to oneself" that count as sexual in addition suggest that there is a privacy inherent in sex acts. In their form, sex acts are "world excluding": custom and taboo aside, sexual arousal and activity, like the activities of reading a poem or praying alone, propel away the ordinary world, the everyday workaday world of public places, public function, and public observation. They do so in several ways.

First, sexually aroused people experience the world in an altered way. Sexual arousal alters perception of reality in some of the same ways powerful drugs do. Space recedes. Arousal is an immersion into a different medium, as into sleep fraught with scary possibilities, or as into a liquid.

In continued arousal, perception becomes more and more focused and narrow. One attends only to what is near. One's gaze no longer roams or scans at large. The focusing process calls for and is enhanced by nightfall. Only what is near, if anything at all, is seen. Gradually, perception is channeled away from vision—the supreme sense of the everyday public world—a sense that requires a gulf of open space between perceiver and perceived. Perception shifts from vision to touch—the sense which requires the absence of open space. At peak arousal, as in a blizzard, the horizon is but the extent of one's flesh. One is hermetic save for the continuation of one's flesh with and in the flesh of another.

No less, sex withdraws one from the world of waking and talking, from reason, persuasion, and thought. Sex is essentially a world of silence; words, such as they are, are not reports, descriptions, or arguments, but murmurs and invocations which emphasize silence and its awe.

Time, like space, recedes with arousal. Suspended is the time by which one gauges the regularity and phases of the workaday world. Time is interrupted and becomes inconsequential, as in the spontaneity and attention-absorbing fascination of games.

Second, social relations alter importantly during the shift into erotic reality; people with whom one has functional, public roles fade away entirely or at least as persons strictly identified with those roles. Colleagues and service personnel fade from consciousness. One becomes focused only upon those who potentially jibe with one's tastes, the particularities of one's erotic choices and desires.

Third, in the process of sexual arousal, one becomes increasingly incarnate, submerged in the flesh. When this process is mutual and paired with the shift in perception to touch, it achieves an unparalleled intimacy. In sexual disengagement from spatial, social, and psychological circumstances, the body ceases to be merely a coathanger for personality. It assumes an independent life of its own.

One perceives the other as flesh and desires the other to be flesh. Usually one becomes, in turn, flesh for another, in part because one's own submersion into the flesh sparks or enhances desire in the other. The recognition of this effect on the other, in turn again, facilitates one's own further submersion. As this process repeats, one eventually becomes just the body sensing. This sexually aroused body, in turn, distills and transforms the sensations typical of the everyday world. A touch, say, a light brushing of the flesh, that would go largely unnoticed in the everyday world, save possibly for its social significance, here becomes an intense yet diffuse pleasure.

Fourth, the everyday world of will and deeds fades away with sexual arousal. The will is not a chief causal factor in the fulfillment of sexual desire. Indeed, quite the opposite is true: the willing of sexual arousal guarantees it will not occur. Sexual arousal must happen *to* one; it is a passion, not an action, project, or deed. It can only occur in situations in which one is not observing one's progress and judging how one is doing. Self-observation, self-judging, and the willing of arousal are the chief causes of—and virtually guarantee—impotence. One has to be lost in the sex for it to work upon one.

The slide into the purely sensing body and the immediacy and simultaneity of touching and being touched produce a transparency in the flow of information and sensation between partners. The vagueness and ambiguity typical of everyday interactions are here refined into a clarity of cause and effect unmatched in human experience. One is as intimate as one could be.

For all the above reasons, the sexual realm is inherently private. The sex act creates its own sanctuary, which in turn is necessary for its success. The whole process and nature of sex is interrupted and destroyed if penetrated by the glance of an intruder. Like the telephone ringing, such observation brings crashing in its train the everyday world of duration and distance, function and duty, will and action. Most importantly, such observation judges—even if sympathetically—causing self-reflection. Such reflection may only generate a sense of uncertainty, but it virtually always causes a great deal more disruption. For, where a socially imposed obligation to maintain an act as private mounts to the level of taboo (as is the case with sex in America), *any* observation, even a seemingly disinterested one, is bound to be construed by the observed as a harsh intrusive judgment. There is no such thing as casual observation of people at rut.

To observe sex, but not participate in it, is to violate the sexual act. Sex's form makes it inherently private. Any moral theory that protects privacy as sanctuary and as repose from the world must presumptively protect sexual activity.

Beyond sex's formal attributes, the function, end, and fulfillment of erotic behavior also provide grounds for thinking that sex is private—private in the sense of "the personal," where the personal means a nonarbitrary, nonidiosyncratic set of central, personally affecting interests. The manner of realizing such central interests is left up to the person who has them, since the personal in this sense is viewed culturally as one's own affair by right. The interests which are the aim, goal, and function of one's erotic choices and behavior meet this level of centrality.

Sexual impulses are directed toward the fulfillment not only of desires but also of needs. Though sexual activity is not necessary to the continued biological existence of an individual, as are some things that are called natural needs, it is a desire (unlike addictions) that recurs independently of its satisfaction. It is a desire that, if one has it at all, constantly presses itself upon life no matter what one does. Taken at face value, sodomy laws block entirely any sex life for gays; in practice they tend more to contribute to social forces that instill guilt into sexual behavior rather than stop sexual behavior. Either way though—through repression or guilt—

sodomy laws curdle and poison the soul. They contribute to people becoming harsh, hard, brittle, obsessive, and alienated. The intrusiveness and perpetual return of sexual desire means that for a healthy personality, the total forgoing of a sex life would itself have to be a major life commitment, possible only if the resignation were itself voluntary—as in the case of nuns and priests, for whom vows of chastity are as central as any vows they take. Mere external restraint could never produce "virtue" here.

Yet, it is not merely as a need that sexual pleasure is central to human life; in intensity and in kind it is unique among human pleasures. It has no passable substitute from other realms of life. For ordinary persons—not mystics or adolescent poets—orgasmic sex is the only access they have to ecstasy. This may take a number of forms: self-transcendence, a "standing outside of self" (which is ecstasy's etymological sense); melting and fusion; engulfing embrace; quiet peace; and self-negation, or what the French euphemistically call an orgasm—"the little death." All of these modes of ecstasy have clear counterparts only in religious visions of the end of life and the ends of life. If pleasure is its own bottom, then sex as the most intense of pleasures is one of the central freestanding components of the good life. Not only must sex be central as a need, it ought to stand centrally as what for most persons causes them to feel the most alive.

Further, if marital love is central to the good life, sex will be central for this reason as well. The relation of sex to love is like the relation of a figured bass to a piece of music with a figured bass or, more so, the repeating bass line of a passacaglia to the passacaglia as a whole, providing the piece both its harmonic and melodic materials, its depth and pulse.

Sex is a necessary part and positive contribution to marital relations; it supports and shapes the whole as a foundation does a house. And this is why friendships for whatever their emotional and spiritual intensity lack the warmth and depth of love relationships. Even if only as possible or recollected, sex acts are the pedal points and diapason of love relationships. This recognition is the kernel of truth left in the religious belief that a marriage unconsummated is not a marriage at all. In blocking gays from having sex, the state would also deny them love. The importance of sex to the good life should make it clear that privacy in sexual matters is central to a person's right to the pursuit of happiness.

Traditionally, sex was thought properly to occur only within marriage; this chapter has suggested that while sex is a prerequisite for a relation to count as marital, sex need not occur within marriage to be worthy of the protection of rights. Traditionally too—and stereotypically—gays have been viewed as interested only in sex, as being emotionally stunted and lacking in the emotional registers of marriage. The next chapter casts doubts on this view, as it looks at the relation between gays and marriage.

CHAPTER 3

Understanding Gay Marriage

The climax of Harvey Fierstein's 1979 play *Torch Song Trilogy* is a dialogue—well, shouting match—between mother and son about traditional marriage and its gay variant. As is frequently the case, the nature and function of an institution flashes forth only when the institution breaks down or is dissolved—here by the death of Arnold's lover.

Arnold: [I'm] widow-ing.
....

Ma: Wait, wait, wait, wait, wait. Are you trying to compare my marriage with you and Alan? Your father and I were married for thirty-five years, had two children and a wonderful life together. You have the nerve to compare yourself to that?
....

What loss did you have? . . . Where do you come to compare that to a marriage of thirty-five years?
....

It took me two months until I could sleep in our bed alone, a year to learn to say "I" instead of "we." Are you going to tell me you were "widowing." How dare you!

Arnold: You're right, Ma. How dare I. I couldn't possibly know how it feels to pack someone's clothes in plastic bags and watch the garbage-pickers carry them away. Or what it feels like to forget and set his place at the table. How about the food that rots in the refrigerator because you forgot how to shop for one? How dare I? Right, Ma? How dare I?

Ma: May God strike me dead! Whatever I did to my mother to deserve a child speaking to me this way. The disrespect! . . .

Arnold: Listen, Ma, you had it easy. You have thirty-five years to remember, I have five. You had your children and friends to comfort you, I had me! My friends didn't want to hear about it. They said "What're you gripin' about? At least you had a lover." 'Cause everybody knows that queers don't feel nothin'. How dare I say I loved him? You had it easy, Ma. You lost your husband in a nice clean hospital, I lost mine out there. They killed him there on the street. Twenty-three years old, laying dead on the street. Killed by a bunch of kids with baseball bats. Children. Children taught by people like you. 'Cause everybody knows that queers don't matter! Queers don't love! And those that do deserve what they get! . . .

Reality concurs with Fierstein's fictional account.

Years of domesticity made Brian and Ed familiar figures in the archipelago of middle-aged middle-class couples who make up my village's permanent gay male community. Ed drives a city bus. Brian was a lineman for the power company until a freak accident set aflame the cherry-picker atop which he worked. He tried to escape by leaping to a nearby tree, but lost his grip and landed on his head. Eventually, it became clear that Brian would be permanently brain-damaged. After a few awkward weeks in the hospital, Brian's parents would not let Ed visit anymore. Eventually they moved Brian to their village and home, where Ed is not allowed.

America has witnessed a similar, famous case: In Minnesota, Karen Thompson fought a legal battle for nearly a decade to gain custody of her lover, Sharon Kowalski, who was damaged of body and mind in a 1983 car accident, after which Kowalski's parents barred Karen from seeing her. What made national headlines out of a Minnesota tragedy is everyday stuff in gay and lesbian lives. If the government had through marriage allowed the members of each couple to be next-of-kin for each other, Sharon and Karen's story and Brian and Ed's story would have had different endings—conclusions in keeping with our cultural belief that those to whom we as adults entrust our tendance in crisis are people we *choose,* our spouses, who love us because of who we are, not people who are thrust upon us by the luck of the draw and who may love us only in spite of who we are.

Consider two other stories. On their walk back from their neighborhood bar to the Victorian which, over the years, they have lovingly restored, Warren and Mark stop along San Francisco's Polk Street to pick up milk for breakfast and Sebastian, their geriatric cat. Just for kicks, some wealthy teens from the Valley drive into town to "bust some fags." Warren dips into a convenience store, while Mark has a smoke outside. As Mark turns to acknowledge Warren's return, he is hit across the back of the head with a baseball bat. Mark's blood and vomit splash across Warren's face. At San Francisco General, Mark is dead on arrival. Subsequently in 1987, a California appellate court holds that

under no circumstance can a relationship between two homosexuals—however emotionally significant, stable, and exclusive—be legally considered a "close relationship," and so
Warren is barred from bringing any suit against the bashers
for negligently causing emotional distress, let alone for
wrongful death.

Mike and Fabo are not your all-American boys. But they
love each other, hold themselves out to the world as a couple,
and have maintained a flat for years in the Mission district.
Mike is an underemployed classicist—Ph.D. Princeton. Fabo
is an underemployed woodworker. In his spare time, he
carves whimsical figurines for neighborhood kids. Mike and
Fabo make ends meet by selling cocaine to yuppies. The
police bungle the drug bust, but Fabo is convicted anyway
based on testimony that the state coerces from Mike. While
Fabo is in prison, Mike dies of AIDS. Had they been allowed
to marry, the testimony could not have been legally coerced—and they would have borne life out together even to
the edge of doom.

Gay and lesbian couples are living together as married
people do, even though they are legally barred from getting
married. The injustices contained in the stories above suggest
that this bar deserves a close examination.

If one asks ordinary people what marriage is, they generally
just get tongue-tied. The meaning of marriage is somehow
supposed to be so obvious in our culture, so entrenched and
ramified in daily life, that it is never in need of articulation.
Standard dictionaries, which track and make coherent common usages of terms, are unhelpfully circular. Most com-
monly, dictionaries define marriage in terms of spouses,

spouses in terms of husband and wife, and husband and wife in terms of marriage. In consequence, the various definitions do no positive work in explaining what marriage is and so simply end up rawly assuming or stipulating that marriage must be between people of different sexes.

Legal definitions of marriage fare no better. Most state laws only speak of spouses and do not actually make explicit that people must be of different genders to marry. During the 1970s, gays challenged these laws in four states, claiming that in accordance with common-law tradition, whatever is not prohibited must be allowed, and that if these laws were judicially construed to require different-sex partners, then the laws constituted illegitimate gender discrimination or sexual orientation discrimination. Gays lost all these cases, which the courts treated in dismissive, summary, but revealing fashion.

The courts would first claim that the silence of the law notwithstanding, marriage automatically entails gender difference. The best-known of these cases, *Singer v. Hara* (Washington State 1974), defined marriage as "the legal union of one man and one woman as husband and wife." This definition has become *the* legal definition of marriage, since it has been taken up into the standard law dictionary, *Black's Sixth Edition,* where *Singer* is the only citation given in the article on marriage. Yet, this definition tells us nothing whatever of the content of marriage. First, the qualification "as husband and wife" is simply circular. Since "husband" and "wife" *mean* people who are in a marriage with each other, the definition, as far as these terms go, presupposes the very thing to be defined. So what is left is that marriage is "the legal union of one man and one woman." Now, if the term "legal" here simply means "not illegal," then notice that a kiss after the prom can fit its bill: "the legal union of one man and one woman." We are told nothing of what "the union" is that is supposed to be the heart of marriage. The formulation of the definition serves no other function than to exclude from marriage—whatever it is—the people whom America views as destroyers of the American family, same-sex couples and polygamists: "*one* man and *one* woman." Like the ordinary dictionary definitions, the legal definition does no explanatory work.

Nevertheless, the courts take this definition, turn around, and say that since this is what marriage *means,* gender discrimination and sexual-orientation discrimination are built right into the institution of marriage, and so since marriage itself is okay, so too must be barring same-sex couples from it. Discrimination against gays, they hold, is not an illegitimate discrimination in marriage, indeed it is necessary to the very institution: no one would be married if gays were, for then marriage wouldn't be marriage. It took a gay case to reveal what marriage is, but this case revealed that marriage, at least as it is legally understood, is nothing but an empty space, delimited only by what it excludes—gay couples. And so this case has all the marks of being profoundly prejudicial in its legal treatment of gays.

If we shift from considering the legal definition of marriage to the legal practices of marriage, are there differences of gender that insinuate themselves into marriage, so that botched definitions aside, marriage does after all require that its pairings be of the male-female variety? There used to be major gender-based legal differences in marriage, but these have all been found to be unjust and have gradually been eliminated through either legislative or judicial means. For example, husbands used to have an obligation to take care of their wives' material needs without their wives (no matter how wealthy) having any corresponding obligation to look after their husbands (however poor). Now, though, both spouses are mutually and equally obliged. It used to be that a husband could sell his wife's property without her consent; the wife had no independent power to make contracts. But these laws have not generally been in force since the middle of the last century and are now unconstitutional. It used to be that a husband could *by definition* not rape his wife—one could as well rape oneself, the reasoning went. Now, while laws governing sexual relations between husbands and wives are not identical to those governing relations between (heterosexual) strangers, they are nearly so, and such differences as remain are in any case cast in gender-neutral terms. Wives are legally protected from ongoing sexual abuse from husbands—whatever the nonlegal reality.

Now that gender distinctions have all but vanished from the legal *content* of marriage, there is no basis for the requirement that the legal *form* of marriage unite members of different sexes. The legal definition of marriage—"union of one man and one woman"—though doggedly enforced in the courts, is a dead husk that has been cast off by marriage as a living legal institution.

Perhaps sensing the shakiness of an argument that rests same-sex discrimination solely on a stipulative definition of little or no content, the courts have tried to supplement the supposedly obvious requirement of marital gender disparity with appeals to reproduction. By assuming that "the procreation and rearing of children" is essential to married life, the courts have implicitly given marriage a functional definition designed to eliminate lesbians and gay men from the ranks of the marriageable. "As we all know" (the courts self-congratulatorily declare), lesbians are "constitutionally incapable" of bearing children by other lesbians, and gay men are incapable of siring children by other gay men.

But the legally acknowledged institution of marriage in fact does not track this functional definition. All states allow people who are over sixty to marry each other, with all the rights and obligations that entails, even though by natural necessity such marriages will be sterile. In Hawaii the statute that requires women to prove immunity against rubella as a condition for getting a marriage license exempts women "who, by reason of age or other medically determined condition, are not and never will be physically able to conceive children." In 1984, Hawaii also amended its marriage statute to delete a requirement that "neither of the parties is impotent or physically incapable of entering into the marriage state." This statutory latitude belies any claim that the narrow purpose of marriage is "to promote and protect propagation."

The functional definition is too broad as well. If the function of marriage is to bear and raise children in a family context, then the state should have no objection to the legal recognition of polygamous marriages. Male-focused polygamous families have been efficient bearers of children; and the economies of scale afforded by polygamous families also make them efficient in the rearing of children.

So given the actual scope of legal marriage, reproduction

and child rearing cannot be its purpose or primary justification. This finding is further confirmed if we look at the rights and obligations of marriage, which exist independently of whether a marriage generates children and which frequently are not even instrumental to childbearing and rearing. While mutual material support might be viewed as guarding the interests of children, other marital rights, such as the immunity against compelled testimony from a spouse, can hardly be grounded in child-related purposes. Indeed, this immunity is waived when relations with one's own children are what is at legal stake, as in cases of alleged child abuse.

The assumption that child rearing is a function uniquely tethered to the institution of heterosexual marriage also collides with an important but little acknowledged social reality. Many lesbian and gay male couples already are raising families in which children are the blessings of adoption, artificial insemination, surrogacy, or prior marriages. The country is experiencing something approaching a gay and lesbian baby boom. Many more gays would like to raise or foster children—perhaps ones from among those alarming numbers of gay kids who have been beaten up and thrown out of their "families" for being gay. A 1988 study by the American Bar Association found that eight to ten million children are currently being raised in three million gay and lesbian households. This statistic, in turn, suggests that around 6 percent of the U.S. population is made up of gay and lesbian families with children. We might well ask what conceivable purpose can be served for these children by barring to their gay and lesbian parents the mutual cohesion, emotional security, and economic benefits that are ideally promoted by legal marriage.

If the desperate judicial and social attempts to restrict marriage and its benefits to heterosexual parents are conceptually disingenuous, unjust, and socially inefficient, what's left of marriage? Should marriage as a legal institution simply be chucked, given the emptiness of its standard justifications? Ought we simply to abandon the legal institution in favor of a family policy that simply and directly looks after the interests of children, leaving all other possible familial relations on the same legal footing as commercial transactions?

Not quite; but to see what's left and worth saving, we need to take a closer look at the social realities of marriage. Currently marriage operates as a legal institution that defines and creates social relations. The law creates the status of husband and wife; it is not a reflection of or response to spousal relations that exist independently of law. This notion that the law "defines and creates social relations" can be clarified by looking at another aspect of family law, one which ordinary people might well find surprising, even shocking. If Paul consensually sires a boy and raises the boy in the way a parent does, then we are strongly inclined to think that he is the boy's father in every morally relevant sense. And we expect the law to reflect this moral status of the father. But the law does not see things this way; it does not reflect and respond to moral reality. For if it turns out that at the time of the boy's birth, his mother was legally married not to Paul but to Fred, the boy is declared by law to be Fred's son, and Paul is, legally speaking, a stranger to the boy. If the mother subsequently boots Paul out and denies him access to the child, Paul has no right at all even to explore legally the possibility that he might have some legislated rights to visit the boy—or so the U.S. Supreme Court declared in 1989. Here the law defines and creates the relation of father and son—which frequently, but only ever by legal accident, happens to accord with the moral reality of father and son. Similarly in the eyes of the law, marriage is not a social form that exists independently of the law and that marriage law echoes and manages. Rather, marriage is entirely a creature of the law—or as Hawaii's Supreme Court recently put it: "Marriage is a state-conferred legal partnership status."

If we want to see what's left in the box of marriage, we need to abandon this model of legal marriage as constitutive of a status, and rather look at marriage as a moral reality independent of law, a moral reality that might well be helped or hindered, but not constituted by the law. Further, current legal marriage, at least as conceptualized by judges, with its definitional entanglements with gender and procreation, is likely to distract us from perceiving lived moral reality.

What then is marriage? Marriage is intimacy given substance in the medium of everyday life, the day-to-day. Marriage is the fused intersection of love's sanctity and necessity's demand.

Not all loves or intimate relations count or should count as marriages. Culturally, we are disinclined to think of Great Loves as marriages. Antony and Cleopatra, Tristan and Isolde, Catherine and Heathcliff—these are loves that burn gloriously but too intensely ever to be manifest in a medium of breakfasts and tire-changes. Nor are Americans inclined to consider as real marriages arranged marriages between heads of state who never see each other, for again the relations do not grow in the earth of day-to-day living.

Friendships too are intimate relations that we do not consider marital relations. Intimate relations are ones that acquire the character they have—that are unique—because of what the individuals in the relation bring to and make of it; the relation is a distinctive product of their separate individualities. Thus intimate relations differ markedly from public or commercial transactions, where, say, there is nothing distinctive about your salesclerk that bears on the meaning of your buying a pair of socks from him. The clerk is just carrying out a role, one that from the buyer's perspective nearly anyone could have performed. Still though friendships are star cases of intimate relationships, we do not count them as marriages; for while a person might count on a friend in a pinch to take her to the hospital, friendly relations do not usually manifest themselves through such necessities of life. Friendships are for the sake of fun, and tend to break down when put to other uses. Friendships do not count as marriages, for they do not develop in the medium of necessity's demand.

On the other hand, neither do we count roommates who regularly cook, clean, tend to household chores, and share household finances as married, even though they "share the common necessities of life." This expression is the typical phrase used to define the threshold requirement for being considered "domestic partners" in towns that have registration programs for domestic partners. Neither would we even consider as married two people who were roommates and even blended their finances if that is all their relationship comprised. Sharing the day-to-day is only one ingredient of marriage.

Marriage requires the presence and blending of both necessity and intimacy. Life's necessities are a mixed fortune: on the one hand, they frequently are drag, dross, and cussedness, yet on the other hand, they can constitute opportunity, abidingness, and prospect for nurture. They are the field across which, the medium through which, and the ground from which the intimacies which we consider marital flourish, blossom, and come to fruition.

This required blend of intimacy and the everyday explains much of the legal content of marriage. For example, the required blend means that for the relationship to work, there must be a presumption of trust between partners; and, in turn, when the relationship *is* working, there will be a transparency in the flow of information between partners—they will know virtually everything about each other. This pairing of trust and transparency constitutes the moral ground for the legal right against compelled testimony between spouses, and explains why this same immunity is not extended to (mere) friends.

The remaining vast array of legal rights and benefits of marriage equally well fit this matrix of love and necessity— chiefly by promoting the patient tendance that such life requires (by providing for privacy, nurture, support, persistence) and by protecting against the occasions when necessity is cussed rather than opportune, especially when life is marked by crisis, illness, and destruction.

First and foremost, marriage changes strangers-at-law into next-of-kin with all the rights which this status entails, including the right to enter hospitals, jails, and other places restricted to "immediate family," the right to obtain "family" health insurance and bereavement leave, the right to live in neighborhoods zoned "single family only," and the right to make medical decisions in the event a partner is injured or incapacitated.

Both from the partners themselves and from the state, marriage provides a variety of material supports which ameliorate, to a degree, necessity's unfriendly intervals. Marriage requires mutual support between spouses. It provides income tax advantages, including deductions, credits, improved rates, and exemptions. It provides for enhanced public assistance in times of need. It governs the equitable control, division, acquisition, and disposition of community property. At death, it guarantees rights of inheritance in the absence of wills—a right of special benefit to the poor, who frequently die intestate. For the wealthy, marriage virtually eliminates inheritance taxes between spouses, since spouses as of 1981 can make unlimited untaxed gifts to each other even at death. For all, it exempts property from attachments resulting from one partner's debts. It confers a right to bring a wrongful death suit. And it confers the right to receive survivor's benefits.

Several marital benefits promote a couple's staying together in the face of changed circumstances. These include the right to collect unemployment benefits if one partner quits her job to move with her partner to a new location because the partner has obtained a new job there, and the right to obtain residency status for a noncitizen partner.

Currently lesbians and gay men are denied all of these rights in consequence of being barred access to legal marriages, even though these rights and benefits are as relevant to committed gay relationships as to heterosexual marriages.

In Illinois as in most jurisdictions, deciding the manner in which someone is to be buried is a statutory right of the next-of-kin—and so gay lovers are frequently barred by the deceased's kin from even attending the lover's funeral. Here the injustice of the law rises to the level of cruelty in its blindness to lived values.

The portraits of gay and lesbian committed relationships that emerge from ethnographic studies—Philip Blumstein and Pepper Schwartz's *American Couples* (1983), David McWhirter and Andrew Mattison's *The Male Couple* (1984), and Kath Weston's *Families We Choose* (1991)—suggest that in the way they typically arrange their lives, gay and lesbian couples fulfill the real definition of marriage in an exemplary manner.

In gay relationships, the ways in which the day-to-day demands of necessity are typically fulfilled are themselves vehicles for the development of intimacy. It is true that gay and lesbian relationships generally divide duties between the partners—this is the efficient thing to do, the very first among the economies of scale that coupledom affords. But who does what is in the first instance a matter of personal preference and joint planning, in which decisions are made in part with an eye to who is better at doing any given task and who has free time—say, for ironing or coping with car-dealerships. But adjustments are made in cases where one person is better at most things—or even everything; here the relation is made less efficient for the sake of equality between partners, who willingly end up doing things they would rather not do—not out of a sense of traditionally assigned duty and role, but out of an impulse to help out, a willingness to sacrifice, and a commitment to equality. In these ways, both the development of intimacy through choice and the proper valuing of love are interwoven in the day-to-day activities of gay couples. Choice improves intimacy; it makes sacrifices meaningful and gives love its proper weight.

Nongays and many gays too are mistaken to think that the sacred valuing of love is something that can be imported from the outside, in public ceremonies invoking praise from God or community. Even wedding vows can smack of cheap moral credit, since they are words, not actions. The sacred valuing of love must come from within and realize itself over time through little sacrifices in day-to-day existence. In this way, intimacy takes on weight and shine, the ordinary becomes the vehicle of the extraordinary, and the development of the marital relation becomes a mirror reflecting eternity.

It is more proper to think of weddings with their ceremonial trappings and invocations as *bon voyages* than as a social institution which, echoing the legal institution of marriage, defines and confers marital status. In a gay marriage, the sanctifications that descend instantly through custom and ritual in many heterosexual marriages descend gradually over and through time—and in a way they are better for it. For the sacred values and loyal intimacies contained in a gay marriage are a product of the relation itself; they are truly the couple's own.

If intimate relations of a certain quality provide the content of marriage, what can the law provide to marriage? Why do we need legal marriage? Folk wisdom has it that both love and justice are blind. But they are blind in different ways, ways which reveal possible conflicts and tensions between love and justice in practice.

Justice is blind—blindfolded—so that it may be a system of neutral, impersonal, impartial rules, a governance by laws, not by idiosyncratic, biased, self-interested persons. Principles of justice in the modern era have been confected chiefly with an eye to relations at arm's length and apply paradigmatically to competitions conducted between conflicting interests in the face of scarce resources. Equal respect is the central concern of justice.

Love is blind—blinded by the light—because stutteringly bedazzled by the beloved. In love, we overlook failings in those whom we cherish. And the beloved's happiness, not respect for the beloved, is love's central concern.

Within the family, we agree that the distribution of goods should be a matter of feeling, care, concern, and sacrifice rather than one conducted by appeal to impartial, impersonal principles of equity. Indeed if the impersonal principles of justice are constantly in the foreground of familial relations, intimacy is destroyed. If every decision in a family requires a judicial-like determination that each member got a fair share, then the care, concern, and love that are a family's breath and spirit are dead. We do not want justice front and center in family life.

But love may lead to intolerable injustices, even as a side effect of one of its main virtues. In the blindness of love, people will love even those who beat them and humiliate them, and those who beat and humiliate others will feel free to do so, or more free to do so, to a family member than to a stranger exactly because the family is the realm of love rather than of civic respect. Some of these humiliations are even occasioned by the distinctive opportunities afforded by traditional family life—in particular, society's misguided notion that everything that occurs behind the family's four walls is private, and so beyond legitimate inquiry.

Conflicts between love and justice can be relieved if we view marriage as a legal institution that allows for appeals to justice when they are needed. We do not want justice to be the motivation for loving relations, but neither do we want love and family to exist beyond the reach of justice. We want justice to be a reliable background and foundation for family life. We therefore need to look at legal marriage as a nurturing ground for social marriage, and not (as now) as that which legally defines and creates marriage and so precludes legal examination of it. We want marriage law to be a conduit for justice in moments of crisis—in financial collapse, in illness, at death—to guard against exploitation both in general and in the distinctive forms that marriage allows.

And indeed family law reform has generally been moving in this direction. Marriage is an evolving institution, not an eternal verity. As noted, inequitable distributions of power by gender have been all but eliminated as a legally enforced part of marriage. In the past and now, people at the margins of society have frequently provided the beacon for reform in family law. Already by the 1930s, black American culture no longer stigmatized children born out of wedlock, though whites continued to do so. In 1971, the Supreme Court belatedly came to realize that punitively burdening innocent children is profoundly unjust, and subsequently through a series of some thirty Supreme Court cases, illegitimacy has all but vanished as a condition legally affecting children born out of wedlock. Further, black Americans provided to the mainstream the model of the extended family with its major virtue of allowing families to have a certain amount of open texture and play at the joints. In 1977, this virtue too was given constitutional status when the Supreme Court struck down zoning laws that barred grandchildren from living with their grandparents, laws which discriminated against extended, typically black, families.

Studies have found that virtually all gay men and lesbians express a desire to have a permanent lover. But currently society and its discriminatory impulse make gay coupling very difficult. It is hard for people to live together as couples without having their sexual orientation perceived in the public realm, which in turn targets them for discrimination. Sharing a life in hiding is even more constricting than life in a nuclear family. Members of nongay couples are here asked to imagine what it would take to erase every trace of their own sexual orientation for even just one week. Still, even against oppressive odds, gays have shown an amazing tendency to nest. And those lesbian and gay male couples who have survived the odds show that the structure of more usual couplings is not a matter of destiny, but of personal responsibility. The so-called basic unit of society turns out not to be a unique immutable atom, but can adopt different parts and be adapted to different needs.

Gay life, like black culture, might even provide models and materials for rethinking and improving family life. I close this chapter by charting some ways in which this might be so—in particular drawing on the distinctive experience and ideals of gay male couples. Lesbian legal theorists have generally supposed marriage too sexist an institution to be salvaged, and lesbian moral theorists too have found traditional forms of coupling highly suspect. Some recommend communal arrangements as the ideal for lesbians; others have proposed that lovers should not even live together. So I shall concentrate on relations between men.

Take sex. Traditionally, a commitment to monogamy—to the extent that it was not simply an adjunct of property law, a vehicle for guaranteeing property rights and succession—was the chief mode of sacrifice imposed upon or adopted by married couples as a means of showing their sacred valuing of their relation. But gay men have realized that while sexual sacrifice may be part of the sacrifices that a couple choose to make in order to show their love for each other, it is not necessary for this purpose; there are many other ways to demonstrate mutual love. Monogamy is not an essential component of love and marriage. In *The Male Couple* McWhirter and Mattison found that "the majority of [gay male] couples, and *all* of the couples together for longer than five years, were not continuously sexually exclusive with each other. Although many had long periods of sexual exclusivity, it was not the ongoing expectation for most. We found that gay men *expect* mutual emotional dependability with their partners [but also believe] that relationship fidelity transcends concerns about sexuality and exclusivity." The law should acknowledge this possibility more generally. Indeed, half the states have decriminalized adultery.

Other improvements that take their cue from gay male couplings might include a recognition that marriages change over time, go through stages, evolve. *The Male Couple* distinguishes six stages that couples typically pass through: blending (year one), nesting (years two and three), maintaining (years four and five), building (years six though ten), releasing (years eleven through twenty), and renewing (beyond twenty years). Relations initially submerge individuality, and emphasize equality between partners, though the equality usually at first takes the form of complementarity rather than similarity. With the passage of years individuality reemerges. Infatuation gives way to collaboration. The development of a foundational trust between the partners and a blending of finances and possessions, interestingly enough, occurs rather late on—typically after ten years. While the most important factor in keeping men together over the first ten years is finding compatibility, the most important factor for the second decade is a casting off of possessiveness, even as the men's lives become more entwined materially and by the traditions and rituals they have established. That relations evolve makes the top-down model of legal marriage as creator of relations particularly inappropriate for human life. Currently at law, the only recognition that marriages change and gather moral weight with time, is the vesting of one spouse's (typically the wife's) interests in the other's Social Security benefits after ten years of marriage. More needs to be explored along these lines. For example, one spouse's guaranteed share of the other's inheritance might rise with the logging of years, rather than being, as in most states, the same traditionally fixed, one-third share, both on day one of the marriage and at its fiftieth anniversary. Men's relations also suggest, however, that the emphasis that has been put on purely material concerns, like blended finances, as the marks of a relation in domestic partnership legislation and in a number of gay family law cases is misguided and fails to understand the dynamics and content of gay relations.

In gay male relations, the relation itself frequently is experienced as a third element or "partner" over and above the two men. This third element frequently has a physical embodiment in a home, business, joint avocation, or companion animal, but also frequently consists of joint charitable, civil, political, or religious work. The third element of the relation both provides a focus for the partners and relieves some of the confining centripetal pressures frequently found in small families. Whether this might have legal implications deserves exploration—it certainly provides a useful model for small heterosexual families.

All long-term gay male relationships, *The Male Couple* reports, devise their own special ways of making the relations satisfying: "Their styles of relationship were developed without the aid of visible role models available to heterosexual couples." This strongly suggests that legal marriage ought not to enforce any tight matrix of obligations on couples if their long-term happiness is part of the law's stake. The law ought rather to provide a ground in which relations can grow and change and recognize their own endings.

Two men clutch each other; one is at the edge of life.

"In sickness and in health."

The other has sold the house to pay the medical bills, changed the hospital sheets himself, sacrificed even beyond the point where assistance could help.

"For richer for poorer."

They are married to each other in their own eyes, in God's eyes, in the eyes of their church and community—in every eye but the law's.

"For better for worse."

And so now, as the doctor unplugs the respirator, as the lovers' duet ends, the law will put the living lover through a hell for which not even his beloved's decay could have prepared his imagination.

"Till death us do part."

CHAPTER 4

Equality

█████████ A student—distraught—slips into the office of her high school guidance counselor. The student thinks she might be a lesbian. It is dawning on her that she seems to like girls rather than boys. And someone has just called her a bad name. The counselor tries to console, advise—counsel—the student to the best of her ability, given available resources. She suggests that being a lesbian is not the end of the world, that she herself, for example, likes women. Buoyed by her success counseling this student and another gay student, the counselor begins to mention her own bisexuality to other school faculty. In consequence, she is fired. After a decade bouncing around the courts, her case reaches the Supreme Court in 1985; but only two justices—half the number needed—even want to hear her case which claims her rights to equal protection have been violated. And so the Court lets stand a ruling that allows Ohio to fire all its gay and lesbian school teachers on the basis of their sexual orientation alone.

This chapter examines how we ought to understand the elusive concept "equal" when used in the Constitution's

cryptic, if moving, promise that "no person shall be denied
the equal protection of the law." It explores the moral background of the country's century-old belief that governments,
both state and federal, should not be allowed to discriminate
and tries to determine whether the constitutional promise of
equality should be extended to include the protection of
gays—as it currently does not. The next chapter examines
the country's more recent belief that the private sector (private employers, hotels, restaurants, and the like) should also
be barred from discriminating against certain groups and
explores whether legislation barring such discrimination
should encompass gays.

The task of this chapter is not an easy one. For it requires
answering the contested questions: What do we mean by
equality anyway? What counts as discrimination? Are gays
relevantly like other minority groups—blacks, the Irish,
women, Jews, the handicapped, Mormons, and others—traditionally thought deserving of protection from governmental discrimination? And for that matter, what is a "minority"?

The stakes for gays are as high as these questions are tough.
For as noted in earlier chapters, governments deny gays
many benefits that they afford to others. They bar gays from
marrying. They frequently discriminate against gays in many
lines of public employment, including state and local jobs
like being a teacher, firefighter, and police officer and in
occupations requiring state licenses. Discrimination is toler-
ated and sometimes even mandated in many federal lines of
employment, including the military, the CIA, the FBI, and
other intelligence agencies. And as we have seen, state sodomy laws too discriminate against gays.

I suggest that equality in a moral sense is at heart a principle that asserts individuals as having equal dignity or personhood. Rising to the level of a right, equality is the authoritative claim that people will not be held in lesser regard, as morally lesser beings, independently of their actions. A person may be held in lower regard, even contempt, because of some action he or she performs—say, lying, thieving, murdering—which both permits and warrants censure and punishment. But a person may not legitimately be held in lower regard because of some status he or she has, some group membership independent of any action that puts the person in the group.

Equality at its core does not merely hold that one should treat similar cases similarly, that people should have equal access to whatever (other) rights there are. This formal principle is a component of procedural justice, but it does not exhaust or even capture the core of equality. Indeed if this were all equality is, equality would simply collapse into freedom. For the very idea of rights entails that their free exercise cannot be granted to some people but not others.

As odd as it probably sounds at first hearing, equality cannot only or essentially mean equality of opportunity, though talk of "equality of opportunity" is quite entrenched in America's folk rhetoric of justice and even in its institutional titles. The chief federal agency for the enforcement of the 1964 Civil Rights Act, for example, is called the Equal Employment Opportunity Commission.

Equality means something more. Consider the following paradigmatic racist joke taken from the second of many volumes of Blanche Knott's best-selling *Truly Tasteless Jokes:* "What do you call a black millionaire physicist who's just won the Nobel Prize? Answer: Nigger!" Here the incongruity which is the basis of the joke's supposed fun is that while the joke's subject through his actions has achieved the pinnacle of socially measured success, still he is viewed as a lesser, even naturally debased, being. The joke turns on the presumed (white) listener's supposing that the person's race makes him in some crucial sense unequal—assigns him a status, a grade of existence, immeasurably lower than that of the average person, the listener, even though his accomplishments are infinitely higher.

The joke is revelatory for understanding equality. First, the structure of the joke's humiliating fun shows that equality cannot chiefly mean equality of opportunity. The person in the joke has availed himself of and realized opportunity as fully as anyone could. The joke's butt could not launch a suit against the joke's teller claiming that he had been denied access to some right, some freedom, some opportunity—for he has it all. Rather the joke presumes that true equality is a consequence of one's status and has nothing to do with one's actions. In the joke's moral system, which is to say America's popular morality, this person could never be equal no matter what he did.

Second, the joke shows that the lesser status which inequality assigns its object is a devolution away from the standard of full personhood. Here race eliminates the subject of the joke from being viewed fully as a person—that is, as an individual with ends of his own, the ability to revise those ends, and the ability to respect others as having ends of their own. The subject is viewed rather as at best an object, tool, or thing. In the moral dynamics of this joke, the black person is merely an instrument for others' entertainment, like a porpoise at Sea World.

This same moral vision was espoused by the Supreme Court in 1857 when it upheld the moral acceptability of slavery, claiming that blacks are an "unfortunate race . . . [correctly] regarded as being of an inferior order, and altogether unfit to associate with the white race, either in social or political relations; and so far inferior, that they had no rights which the white man was bound to respect; that the negro might justly and lawfully be reduced to slavery for his own benefit." Although slavery is, like a tax too high, an unjust restriction on liberty, the chief moral problem with slavery is that it is a violation of equality. An injury, a harm, or a restriction to one's freedom may interrupt one's ability to carry out one's life plan, but an assault on equality, viewed as individual dignity, presumes that one is not even the sort of thing to deserve the status of having a life plan of one's own. To be treated inequitably is to be held in morally lesser regard independently of what one has done. It is to suffer degradation, humiliation, indignity.

Now admittedly, dignity is an elusive notion. Nevertheless, the common phrase "adding insult to injury" affords an intuitive grasp of the relevant distinction between two types of evil. An insult is an offense against dignity, while an injury is something that reduces one's happiness, denies one some benefit, wealth, power, or useful possession, or generally reduces one's material circumstances in the world.

This distinction is reflected in the different moral emotions we feel toward those whose well-being or dignity is of interest to us. The moral emotion that has happiness and harm as its proper objects is sympathetic concern—sympathetic joy or sympathetic pity. But we feel sympathetic concern, even love, for things which are not full persons, for example, pets.

In contrast, the moral feeling appropriate for dignity is not sympathy, but respect. If our regard for others does not include respect, we fail to treat them as persons, and treat them instead as lesser beings. Insults are a graver form of evil than injuries, for they attack persons as persons—in two ways. First, by focusing importance on largely irrelevant characteristics, insults attack persons as repositories of deserved fair treatment and equal respect. The most common indignities—invective and name-calling, insults in a narrow sense—attack a person without regard to anything that he or she has done. Thus insults such as calling someone a "nigger," "faggot," or "cunt" violate their target's right to equal respect in that the insulted person's ability to formulate and carry out a plan of life—to realize her desires, plans, aspirations, and sense of the sacred—is not considered worthy of social care and concern on a par with that of others.

Second, by holding a person in morally diminished regard, insults show disrespect for persons as moral agents. Respect for moral agency is violated because these persons are being judged without regard to their individual merits or accomplishments. In this way, invective and insult demote people to the level of children, animals, or trees, things which are not held responsible as makers of their own destinies.

The ill-treatment of gays chiefly takes the form of denials of equality. To be sure, gays are subject to violations of freedom and inflictions of severe harms. Still, these violations and inflictions are usually perpetrated chiefly as vehicles for the denial of equality to gays. Being fired or being physically attacked because one is gay is a harm, but even more so it is a degradation. Gay oppression is mainly the denial of gay dignity.

A look in some detail at language will perhaps provide the most telling complex of examples to show that gays in America are indeed viewed and, in turn, treated inequitably—as a group degraded independently of any behavior that makes one a member of the group.

Surprisingly, even nonslang terms used to denote gays preponderantly indicate that society does not think of gays as defined by certain kinds of acts. Dictionaries' trackings of common usage and their definitions of "homosexual" reveal much. The *Oxford English Dictionary* (1964) defines "homosexual" simply and solely as "having a sexual propensity for persons of one's own sex." Similarly *Webster's New Twentieth Century* (1952) has for the adjective "characterized by sexual inclination toward the same sex," and for the noun "one whose emotions, feelings, and desires are concerned with the individual's own sex rather than with the opposite sex." No mention of actions is made here. Actions are not necessary for the label to apply to a person. Nor, importantly, are actions here even sufficient for the label to apply. For one can, and quite often does, will and perform actions without having a desire, inclination, propensity, or (positive) feeling for the actions performed—carrying out arduous tasks and undergoing major surgery are actions of this sort.

These definitions of "homosexual" do indeed conform with ordinary American usage and social practice. Tellingly, the formulations of the U.S. Armed Forces' policies on homosexuality developed in the 1980s followed the dictionary

view that engaging in homosexual behavior is neither a necessary nor sufficient cause for being considered a homosexual and treated accordingly. In these formulations, homosexual desire (as expressed, say, in a diary entry) is, even in the
absence of any behavior, sufficient to have one kicked out
of the armed forces for homosexuality; yet if a member of
the military is caught actually performing homosexual sex
acts, he is permitted to plead successfully that these do not
indicate his true nature and that "such conduct is a depar-
ture from the member's usual and customary behavior." One
may claim "Just skylarking," or "Boy, was I drunk last night,"
and be retained. Clearly in these formulations, it is one's
status as a homosexual—a status that can float completely
separate from any behavior—that is the brunt of military
policy.

Anti-gay slurs in American English also target a person's
status rather than behavior. With the apparent exception of
"cocksucker," no widespread anti-gay slur gives any indica-
tion that its censure is directed at sex acts rather than despised social status. Group-directed slurs (dyke, queer, fag)
place gays in a significant social category along with blacks
(nigger, shine, shitskin), other racial groups (chink), women
(cunt, gash), various ethnic groups (wop, dago, gook, jap,
JAP, mick, kike), religious groups (kike, papist, christer),
native peoples (redskin, injun, eskimo), nonnative peoples
(kike, gypsy), and the physically challenged (crip, gimp, veg,
vegetable, crispy critter). They do not place gays in the same
category as liars, hypocrites, murderers, and thieves—those
who commit immoral and criminal actions and yet for whom
culture in no case has coined group-based invectives. This

schema of slurs strongly suggests that gays are held to be immoral because they are hated, rather than hated because they are immoral.

Many slang pejoratives explicitly denote homosexual status rather than homosexual acts. The whole host of put-downs of gay men nominally based on charges of effeminacy are of this sort. They put down gay men not as performers of sodomy but as having a low status derivative from the low status in which society holds women, and additionally from the sense that they have betrayed their socially assigned gender-status. To be sure, betrayal is a willful action, but here it is not the willfulness of being a "quean" that is the brunt of slurs like "sissy" and "nelly." It is the challenge which the quean's status presents to socially managed gender distinctions that is condemned. Hence the condemnation of will is inextricably bound up with the protection of status—the quean's very existence is a challenge to the status "real manhood." Action has little to do with the perceived threat.

Similarly, slang which calls lesbians truckdrivers, bulldykes, and the like are put-downs based on the betrayal of status. But the thrust of the charge against lesbians is less intense for the betrayal involved is not a threat to manhood—which society views as a fixed natural attribute, from which a male may perversely depart but to which no one other than a male may aspire. The perversity of bulldykes is that they, like "uppity niggers," "strident women," and "flaunting faggots," are trying to rise above their naturally assigned station and status. Their betrayal is the betrayal of womanhood and its "proper" place. Perhaps contrary to some liberal intuitions, a 1980 empirical study in the *Journal of Homosexuality* titled "Why Lesbians are Disliked" found that women in general both disliked "butch" lesbians more and viewed them as more of a threat than men did. So again, status is primary, and the willfulness of the betrayal is derivative.

A useful probe for determining whether a complex social classification, like effeminacy or butchness, has been made with respect to status, not actions, is to imagine whether for the class one could draw demarcations that capture the individuals of the class one by one, without first treating the class as a social grouping and only then being able to pick out its members. Take hippies, for example. For every action that one might think definitive of a hippie (smoking pot, wearing "weird" clothes, etc.), one can find some other group that performs that action, but which is not put down as a group by reference to that action. What (middle-class) society didn't like about hippies was the whole package, their whole complex of attitudes and behaviors—in short, a status—which itself could never pass muster for assigning, say, individual criminal accountability. So even though being a hippie, like being a member of a religion, is a matter of choice, still hippies were despised not as failed moral agents, but as bearers of a degenerate status.

In these circumstances, any particular part of the bundle that makes up the despised status, a part that might be specific and reasonably lamented enough even to be criminal (say, smoking pot), is nevertheless despised not for what it is on its own, but as a marker for or sign of the package as a whole, a sign of the status. And such appeal to the part is an illegitimate source of censure, for the value placed on it is entirely parasitic upon the illegitimate treatment of persons as having a group status.

The Pentagon's 1993 regulations barring open gays from

the Armed Services provide a good example of the relation between markers and despised status. The regulations disingenuously claim to discriminate solely on the basis of homosexual acts and not at all on the basis of homosexual status. What counts, though, as homosexual acts is decidedly odd. Goings-on for which a soldier is to be dismissed include holding hands, dancing, and kissing: "Bodily contact between service members of the same sex that a reasonable person would understand to demonstrate a *propensity* or intent to engage in homosexual acts will be *sufficient* to initiate separation." But these actions are simply markers of sexual orientation status—as the word "propensity" more or less admits—rather than acts which are despised and censurable independently of reference to despised sexual orientation status. For if these actions, without more, were considered sexual acts, we would not allow parents to perform them with their children, as in fact we do. The discriminatory impulse here remains entirely parasitic upon despised status. These are homosexual acts only in that despised homosexuals perform them.

Similarly, the new policy's ideology would have us believe that saying that one is gay is itself an act of sex. This is quite bizarre. It is as good to hold that saying that one wants to kill someone is itself an act of murder. If this were so, we'd all be in jail. In actual practice, the policy treats saying that one is gay neither as a sexual act nor even as a true report of sexual actions (say, as evidence for a sodomy prosecution), but as a stand-in or symbol for a status against which the policy discriminates. Again sexual orientation alone is the brunt of the discrimination.

This use of markers to indicate status also explains the use of "cocksucker" to degrade gay men. The term seems to have a sex act as its content and so might well seem to have behavior, not status, as the target of its derision. But in truth, the charge "cocksucker" has as little to do with sucking cock as the charge "motherfucker" has to do with fucking one's mother. "Cocksucker" stands to male homosexuality as "mackerel-eater" stands to Catholicism. In both cases, the name of an action (sucking, eating) is used as a code for a status. We know this for sure in the case of "cocksucker," because the term is never used as an aspersion cast against women who suck cock, just as "mackerel-eater" is never used against Protestants who happen to eat mackerel.

Similarly, assuming for the sake of argument that effeminacy among some gay men and butchness among some lesbians is chosen, not congenital, still effeminacy and butchness are each, like being a hippie, a complex characteristic which cannot be given a clear enough characterization to be counted as culpable action, and such actions as are part of its make-up do not even have enough independent moral life to justify censure of them. The component parts of the status—say, a limp wrist and a swinging gait or wearing flannel and smoking stogies—are distinctively and immediately despised not on their own as possibly blameworthy acts but because they, like "hippie behavior," are signs or markers for a despised status. What the effeminate male and butch lesbian does does not matter. It is their mere existence, mere presence, that offends. Such acts as gays are thought to perform—whether sexual, gestural, or social—are viewed socially as the expected or even necessary efflorescence of gays' lesser moral state, of their status as lesser beings, rather than as the distinguishing marks by which they are defined as a group. Such purported acts—the stuff of stereotypes—provide the materials for a retrospectively constructed ideology concocted to justify the group's despised status, just as, for instance, the beliefs that Jews poison wells and kill babies and messiahs are concocted, as socially "needed," to justify society's hatred of Jews. Hatred's targeting of status is primitive, and its condemnation of behavior an ideologically inspired afterthought.

Another large set of slurs explicitly denote status in their metaphoric vehicles, and thus suggest that their target—male homosexuality—is also being viewed as a status. These slurs include: pansy, panz, fruit, fruitcake, and *finocchio* (Italian for fennel and the name of a decades-old Sausalito transvestite bar). These slurs, which have no lesbian counterparts or analogues, obviously make no reference to behavior of any kind. All of them derive from the cosmic order "vegetable," and vegetables don't do anything. Rather these slurs suggest that America's mind believes in a Great Chain of Moral Being. Straight men—fully real persons—constitute the highest tier of all the gradations of human moral worth. Of sublunar beings, they are nearest the ascending heavenly hierarchy of saints, cherubim, seraphim, archangels, and gods. Descending down the chain from real men, we arrive next at women, whose nature is essentially, abidingly, and pervasively viewed in slang as animal. Women are chiefly referred to in slurs by designations of animal species (bitch, beaver, cow, fish, vixen, pussy, shrew), by terms which assimilate women to immature animals and children (chick, babe, baby), or which reduce women to the body parts by which their animality differs from that of males (cunt, gash, beaver, pussy, bag, muff, cow, tit-rack). Note that there are no corresponding derogatory terms for males in contemporary culture. The derogatory terms that have male genitalia as their metaphoric vehicles—prick, dickhead—are not in fact put-downs of men as men, but are simply equivalents to "bozo" or "dolt." Real men are unassailable. Their antipode down at the bottom of the human heap is vegetable existence—pansies, fruits, *and* the physically challenged, who, like gay men, also are typically denoted and demoted with vegetative slurs. The lowly placement of gay men on a scale which contains women, men, and the congenitally deformed shows that the social treatment of gay men depends not upon what they do, but upon some perceived degenerate status.

Quite generally then, it would appear that when animosity against some group reaches a level where the group is the subject of highly developed, sharply derisive slang and the butt of vicious jokes, then the group's members are not being held accountable for what they do but for what they are. At present society chooses to treat gays not as agents of their own destiny with respect to their group designation, but simply as having a degenerate status for the designation of which actions and responsibility are irrelevant.

In addition to the linguistic record, much more and diverse evidence shows that in lopsided preponderance society views gays first and foremost simply as morally lesser beings. In the mid-1980s two major institutions—religion and medicine—weighed in to affirm the moral model that classifies gays by status rather than by actions.

Religion: In 1986, the Catholic church, in a major ideological shift, branded as "an objective moral disorder" the mere status of being a homosexual, even when congenitally fixed and unaccompanied by any homosexual behavior. Previously such status had been held morally neutral and only homosexual acts were morally censured. Both the Vatican letter stating this shift and a 1992 Vatican letter interpreting it as warranting employment discrimination against gays seemed, by their wording and the way they framed issues, to be a specific response to the development of gay politics in the United States. Political stirring produced ideological retrenchment, in a way, though, that tipped religion's hand and revealed its anti-gay stance.

Medicine: On April 15, 1985, in Atlanta during the keynote address for the first International Conference on AIDS, President Reagan's Secretary of Health and Human Services, Margaret Heckler, in a burst of good intentions gone painfully awry, held: "We must conquer AIDS before it affects the heterosexual population . . . the general population. We have a very strong public interest in stopping AIDS before it spreads outside the risk groups, before it becomes an overwhelming problem." The determinate prospect of a million or so dead gay men was not seen as a problem by the Reagan administration. Now, in America the value assigned to an individual's life is not normally distinguished with respect to the means by which that person comes to have a disease. For instance, the life of a C.E.O. who suffers a heart attack from years of gluttony is not thought to be worth less than that of a person who suffers a heart attack under torture. So even if one drew a moral distinction between the AIDS-conveying sex acts of heterosexuals and those of homosexuals, still this would not ground a further distinction between lives to be saved and lives to be junked. So further it is not the moral assessment of actions which grounds

Heckler's distinction; rather she holds heterosexual status as more worthy of care and concern than gay status. Gays, here, are lesser beings.

The social understanding of homosexuality essentially as a degenerate status rather than as a form of censurable behavior has been given its most clear and honest formulation in this century by Heinrich Himmler, who, in a speech to his SS generals, explained that the medieval German practice of drowning male homosexuals in bogs "was no punishment, merely the extermination of an abnormal life. It had to be removed just as we [now] pull up stinging nettles, toss them on a heap, and burn them."

This understanding of gays as possessing a degenerate status has important consequences for understanding gay men and lesbians as a minority. In its most central, frequent, and important usage, "minority" is a normative rather than a descriptive term. Rare is its use in its descriptive, statistical meaning—"less than 50 percent"—as in "the bill failed because it garnered only a minority of the legislators' votes."

Perhaps surprisingly, "minority" in its normative sense does not even entail the term's descriptive or statistical sense. The expression now found in job advertisements encouraging "women and other minorities to apply" and in federal set-aside programs which count women as a minority shows that the statistical sense of "minority" is not a necessary condition for the correct application of the term taken in its normative sense.

On what then does "being a minority" turn? I think American English, the Catholic church, and Margaret Heckler provide a sufficient clue. A minority is a group treated unjustly because of some status which the group is socially perceived to possess independently of the behavior of the group's members. A "minority" is a group whose members have been treated inequitably. This definition captures the scope and normative force of the term. Thus women, though statistically a majority, are considered a minority, whereas people with blue eyes, though statistically a minority, are not: there are no minority set-aside programs for people with blue eyes. Yet, given this definition, current discussions of gays as a minority have been largely misguided because irrelevant.

Almost all of the popular debate about gays—and a fair amount of the academic debate—has turned on whether being gay is an immutable characteristic. If it is, gays would be, so it is claimed, relevantly like blacks—alike in that one's group characteristic is not of one's own doing, with the result that in a group-based discrimination one is treated unjustly because treated without regard to what one oneself has done. But even if it were conclusively proven that being gay is not a matter of choice, we would have to be careful in drawing conclusions from that fact. For sometimes making social distinctions with respect to nonchosen properties is morally acceptable, even morally to be expected. For example, "grandfathering provisions" are not, in themselves, considered unjust. A law with a grandfathering provision blocks future access to a privilege, but allows those currently granted the privilege (say, a vendor's license or a land use at odds with newly restrictive zoning) to maintain it. If grandfather exceptions do not front for some illegitimate goal (for example, perpetuating racial oppression in the post-Reconstruction era), then they are not felt to be substantially unjust, even though they create closed classes of people with privileges to which others, sometimes simply as a result of when they were born, can have no access no matter what they do. Or again: a law that lowers the inheritance tax rate will disadvantage a person whose parents have already died compared to people whose parents have not yet died. Still this disadvantage is not an injustice to him, even though its falling upon him is not a consequence of anything he has done. All sorts of legitimate state programs and laws give different people differential access to certain opportunities, but this does not automatically mean that they constitute violations of a fundamental right.

When taken as a moral principle, the claim that one is not to be discriminated against with respect to some characteristic over which one has no control has all the usefulness but roughness of a rule of thumb—immutable characteristics *usually* will be morally irrelevant. If a law makes a distinction with reference to an immutable characteristic, it deserves a close second look to make sure that people's immutable characteristics are not being given a moral weight they do not warrant and that the distinction is indeed instrumental to a legitimate government project. But barring that, and as long as the law does not degrade some group, it is morally acceptable. Immutable characteristics are not sufficient conditions for triggering minority status and minority protections.

Neither are immutable characteristics necessary conditions for moral minority status. Among minorities which have properly invoked constitutional protections are religious minorities and the physically challenged *even* when the challenge in question is the result of actions for which the handicapped person himself is responsible, such as negligent driving or a botched suicide. Minority standing that is based only on biological or psychological determinism lets in both too much and too little.

Whether gays are or are not in the eye of nature objectively like a highly distinctive ethnic group, that is how society views and treats them—as a despised ethnic minority and not as a pack of criminals. Society's attitudes toward and treatment of gays, as revealed in its treatment of them in slang and invective, derogatory group-based jokes, stereotypes, group-directed violence, symbolic legislation (such as unenforced sodomy laws), Catholic theology, and health policy, all presuppose and reinforce the moral vision that gays are lesser moral beings.

This treatment justifies the application to gays of the moral sense of minority, and in turn ought to invoke the constitutional norms the culture thinks appropriate for minority status, especially enhanced constitutional equal protections of the sort currently afforded by the Supreme Court to blacks, ethnic minorities, religious minorities, legal aliens, illegal alien children, illegitimate children, women, and the mentally and physically challenged. For the treatment of gays corrupts both the substance and procedures of a constitutionally restrained democracy.

The social degradation of gays and the existence of anti-gay stereotypes, for example, show that the concerns of gays individually are not *substantively* given equal care and concern with the concerns of members of the dominant culture. The needs, desires, and aspirations of gays simply do not command the respect of those who make up the majority and so either do not register at all or are at least devalued in the calculus effected by majority rule in its establishment of social policy. This reason alone is sufficient to show that gays need and deserve constitutional protection from majoritarian decision making, in, for example, school board policies affecting hiring and course content.

Equally important though is that society's treatment of gays tends to short-circuit the standard *procedures* of intelligent public policy making and of justice more generally. Stereotypes and other hostile attitudes toward gays are not chiefly the effects of misperceiving gays, of getting gays wrong. Rather they are what cause the misperception and in turn the mistreatment of gays. Anti-gay stereotypes and the like are not simply illegitimate as factual bases for making social decisions about gay men and lesbians; they are also lenses through which gays are viewed and assessed. Stereotypes become part of a person's cognitive capacities and evaluative apparatus, and so cause misjudgments, with both prejudicial treatment and social inefficiency as their result. Because people are not aware, indeed frequently deny, that they have these judgment-distorting social lenses in their minds, they are frequently prejudiced without intending to be or even knowing that they are being prejudiced. This social fact is extremely important for courts and government administrators to acknowledge, for it greatly distorts hiring decisions and fairness in the administration of criminal and civil justice.

A striking, if disturbing, empirical study reported in the *Journal of Social Issues* for 1978 confirmed that these widely recognized relations between stereotypes and the prejudicial treatment of other minority groups also hold specifically for gays. In it, men who were led to believe another man was homosexual, after interacting with him in group projects, tended to view him far more negatively than when the same man was assumed to be heterosexual. The person labeled homosexual was considered less clean, softer, more "womanly," more tense, more yielding, more impulsive, less rugged, more passive, and quieter. Collectively these characteristics are the contradictory amalgam of effeminacy and threat that are society's main stereotypes of gay males; the characteristics are all ones which a person might use to justify discrimination and to rationalize away prejudice against gay men. But the characteristics were all read into the social interaction, not out of it. The man labeled did not know whether he was labeled homosexual or not. And the study was sufficiently controlled to ensure that any differences in social perception were due to the difference in labeling, not to any change in the behavior of the labeled person.

The study has two additional alarming findings. First, the man who labeled the other as homosexual was viewed more positively for having so labeled the presumed homosexual than when he did not; it appears that one scores social points for accusing someone of being a "fag" whether he is or not. Second, groups of men functioned less efficiently when they believed a homosexual man to be present among them. This feature of the study raises the prospect that openly gay men will be particularly subject to the social dynamics of "blaming the victim," when in fact, as the study showed, social inefficiency rests entirely on the shoulders of those with unacknowledged prejudicial views of gays.

Quite apart from any history of intentional discrimination against gays, the existence of anti-gay stereotypes operating as unacknowledged social lenses in policy making ensures that democratic processes cannot be relied upon to guarantee fair and impartial treatment of gay issues. Indeed the effects of stereotypes in society's judgment-making undercut the very grounds for affirming representational democracy as a form of government. For reasons of the coherence of democratic theory, gays ought to be given enhanced equal protections against discrimination by government.

The natural human responses to injuries and harms are pain and an analogue to pain—the form of anger which is described as being riled up. Proper remedies are compensation and perhaps retribution. The response to insult is not pain and its analogue, but resentment and indignation—an anger that does not lash out in retaliation, but a pure, cool anger. The remedy sought cannot be compensation, for though one person can treat another as less than a person, one person cannot constitute another person as a moral agent. The proper action of the offended party is one that directly reasserts the dignity that was denied—for example, by publicly naming an insult as bigotry—in order to secure that dignity in such a way that it cannot as easily be denied again, even if the person who thus asserts her dignity, by doing so, places herself at risk for harms, say, from a bigoted employer, police officer, or even a friend.

At the level of individual interactions, the goal of such assertion is heartfelt apology from the offender. In America there is a forum for the redress of those assaults to dignity that are perpetrated by government: the courts as expounders of Constitutional rights, especially rights to equal protection. To the extent that anti-gay laws are an assault on dignity and to the extent that dignity is not, as it is not, something which ought morally to depend on the whims of majorities, then the courts are not just an available forum to overturn anti-gay discrimination—they are also the proper forum. Given the inherently political nature of representative bodies, there is no effective equivalent on the social level to an individual's heartfelt apology. There is only the assertion of rights.

CHAPTER 5

Civil Rights

Current federal civil rights law bars private-sector discrimination in housing, employment, and public accommodations on the basis of race, national origin, ethnicity, gender, religion, age, and disability, but not sexual orientation. Where city councils and state legislatures have passed protections for gay men and lesbians, the protections have been under concerted and frequently successful attack through referendum initiatives. Thus in November 1992, Colorado adopted by referendum a state constitutional provision voiding existing city protections for gay men and lesbians and barring any future city or state protections for them. This chapter offers moral arguments for protecting lesbians and gay men from private-sector discrimination.

Even though civil rights legislation restricts somewhat the workings of free enterprise, it promotes other core American values that far outweigh this slight loss of entrepreneurial freedom. These values are self-respect, self-sufficiency, general prosperity, and individual flourishing.

No one in American society can have much self-respect or maintain a solid sense of self, if she is, in major ways affecting herself, subject to whimsical and arbitrary actions of others. Work, entertainment, and housing are major modes through which people identify themselves to themselves. Indeed in modern culture, work and housing rank just after personal relationships and perhaps (for some) religion, as the chief means by which people identify themselves to themselves. A large but largely unrecognized part of the misery of unemployment is not merely poverty and social embarrassment, but also a sense of loss of that by which one defined oneself, a loss which many people also experience upon retirement, even when their income and social esteem are left intact. People thrown out of work frequently compare this loss to the loss of a family member, especially to the loss of a child. Here the comparison is not simply to the intensity of the emotion caused by the loss, but to the nature of the loss: what was lost was a central means by which one constituted one's image of oneself.

Work is also the chief means by which people in America identify themselves to others. Indeed in America, one's job is tantamount to one's social identity. Socially one finds out who a person is by finding out what she or he does. At social gatherings, like parties, asking after a person's employment is typically the first substantive inquiry one makes of a person to whom one has been introduced. America is a nation of doers. When job discrimination is directed at lesbians and gay men, say, as a child care worker or museum director, it is a way of branding them as essentially un-American, as alien. It is a chief mode of expatriation from the national experience.

Discrimination in housing similarly affects one's social identity. The physical separation of a group and its concentration apart from the dominant social order are among the chief means by which a group is socially marked as worthy of less respect, unclean, and threatening. Housing discrimination against a despised group is apartheid writ small, but not small enough to be morally acceptable.

Discrimination in housing also affects one's self-perception. It perhaps goes without saying that the conversion of a house into a home is one of the main aspects of self-definition in America. Blocking or arbitrarily restricting the material basis of this conversion inhibits the development of self-respect and selectively disrupts the sanctities of private life. The common expression "keeping up with the Joneses," even in its mild censure or irony, attests to the role of housing in the way people identify themselves to themselves, in part, through the eyes of others. To be denied housing on the basis of some group status is another chief mode of social ostracism and exile.

In a nonsocialist, noncommunist society like America, there is a general expectation that each person is primarily responsible for meeting his or her own basic needs and that the government becomes an active provider only when all else fails. It is largely noncontroversial that people ought to have their basic needs met. For meeting basic needs is a necessary condition for anyone being able to carry out a life plan. If government aims at enhancing the conditions in which people are able to carry out their life plans, then enhancing the conditions in which basic needs are met will be a high government priority, all the more so if the means to this end themselves avoid greatly coercing people's life plans.

Current civil rights legislation tries to unclog channels between an individual's efforts and the fulfillment of the individual's needs. For it is chiefly through employment, in conjunction with access to certain public accommodations and housing, that people acquire the things they need to assure their continued biological existence—food, shelter, and clothing. Importantly, these are also the chief means by which people satisfy those various culturally relative needs which maintain them as credible players in the ongoing social, political, and economic "games" of the society into which they are born—say, needs for transportation and access to information. Civil rights legislation then helps people discharge their presumptive obligation to meet through their own devices their basic biological needs and other conditions required for human agency.

If gays were barred only from buying rocks at Tiffany's, eating truffles at "21," and holding seats on the Board of Trade, their inclusion in civil rights laws on the ground that such laws help meet needs would not be very compelling. And indeed America holds a stereotype of gays, especially gay men, as wealthy, frivolous, selfish, conspicuous consumers. Based on this stereotype, some people claim that gays are not in need of civil rights protections. But the stereotype is false. One of the surprising findings of Alfred Kinsey's 1948 study of male sexuality was that more male homosexual behavior occurs among the economically disadvantaged and among the uneducated than among the wealthy and college educated. And it is generally acknowledged that lesbians on average fall well below the national average for income, if for no other reason than that women are so far below the national average for income.

One of the little-sung heroes of the gay movement is John F. Singer. On June 26, 1972, Singer was fired from the Equal Employment Opportunity Commission. He was fired for being gay. His case took six years in front of numerous courts and administrative panels before he was vindicated. Along the way, it helped force the federal government to change its administrative policies toward lesbians and gays in civil service jobs. When fired, he held the position of filing clerk.

Extending civil rights protection to gay men and lesbians is also justified as promoting general prosperity. Such legislation tends to increase the production of goods and services for society as a whole. It does so in three ways.

First, by eliminating extraneous factors in employment decisions, such legislation promotes an optimal fit between a worker's capacities and the tasks of her prospective work. Both the worker and her employer are advantaged because a worker is most productive when her talents and the requirements of her job mesh. Across the business community as a whole, such legislation further enhances the prospects that talent does not go wasting and that job vacancies are not filled by second bests.

In response to prospective discrimination, gays are prone to take jobs which only partially use their talents. Many gays take dead-end jobs; they do so in order to avoid reviews which might reveal their minority status and result in their dismissal. Many gay men and lesbians go into small business because big business will not have them. In turn, many small businesses or dead-end occupations, like being a florist, hairdresser, male nurse, female trucker or construction worker, have in society's mind become so closely associated with homosexuality that nongays who might otherwise go into these lines of employment do not do so out of fear that they will be socially branded as gay. In these circumstances, the talents of people—both gay and nongay—are simply wasted both to themselves and to society. Rights for gays are good for everyone.

Second, human resources are wasted if one's energies are constantly diverted and devoured by fear of arbitrary dismissal. The cost of life in the closet is not small, for the closet permeates and largely consumes the life of its occupant. In the absence of civil rights legislation for gays, society is simply wasting the human resources which are expended in the day-to-day anxiety—the web of lies, the constant worry—that attends leading a life of systematic disguise as a condition for continued employment.

Third, employment makes up a large part of what happiness is. To a large extent, happiness is job satisfaction. When one's employment is of a favorable sort, one finds a delight in its very execution—quite independently of any object which the job generates, whether product or wage. People whose work on its own is rich enough and interesting enough to count as a personal flourishing, people, for instance, employed in human services, academics, and other professionals, and people whose jobs entail a large element of craft, like editors and artisans, are indeed likely to view job satisfaction as a major constituent of happiness and rank it high both qualitatively and quantitatively among the sources of happiness. And even people who are forced by necessity or misfortune to take up employment which does not use their talents, or which is virtually mechanical, or positively dangerous, or which has other conditions that make the workplace hateful—even these people are likely to recognize that the workplace, if properly arranged, would be a locus of happiness, and this recognition of opportunity missed is part of the frustration which accompanies jobs which are necessarily unsatisfying to perform. Permitting discriminatory hiring practices reduces happiness generally by barring access to one of its main sources.

Civil rights legislation also promotes individual flourishing—not merely by enhancing the prospect that individuals' needs are met, but more so by expanding the ranges of individual choice. Government has a perceived obligation to enhance conditions which promote the flourishing of individual styles of living. Thus, for example, the general rationale for compulsory liberal education is that such compulsion ultimately issues in autonomous individuals capable of making decisions for themselves from a field of alternative opinions. Analogously, civil rights legislation, though a somewhat coercive force in the marketplace, promotes those conditions that enable people to draw up and carry out their life plans.

Such legislation withdraws the threat of punishment by social banishment, loss of employment, and the like from the arsenal of majoritarian coercion, so that individual lives need not be molded by social conventions and by the demands of conformity set by others. The result of such legislation is that the means by which one lives shall not be permitted to serve as instruments for the despotism of custom.

This justification for civil rights legislation has special import for gay men and lesbians. With the lessening of fear from threat of discovery, ordinary gays will begin to lead self-determining lives. Imagine the lives of those gays who systematically forgo the opportunity of sharing the common necessities of life and of sharing the emotional dimensions of intimacy as the price for the means by which they place bread on their table. Love and caring could cost you your job—if you're gay—while catch-as-catch-can sex and intimacy could cost you your life.

In the absence of civil rights legislation, lesbians and gay men are placed in the position of having to make zero-sum trade-offs between the components that go into making a full life, trade-offs, say, between a reasonable personal life and employment, trade-offs which the majority would not tolerate for themselves even for a minute.

As an invisible minority, gay men and lesbians also need civil rights protections in order for them to have reasonably guaranteed access to an array of fundamental rights which virtually everyone would agree are supposed to pertain equally to all persons.

By "invisible minority," I mean a minority whose members can be identified only through an act of will on someone's part, rather than merely through observation of the members' day-to-day actions in the public domain. Thus severely physically and mentally challenged people would rank along with racial classes, gender classes, and some ethnic and religious groups (like the Amish) as visible minorities, whereas diabetics, assimilated Jews, Lutherans, atheists, and released prisoners would rank along with gay men and lesbians as invisible minorities.

Let us presume the acceptability of a governmental system which is a constitutionally regulated representative democracy with a developed body of civic law. Such in broad outline is the government of the United States and its various states. Then, gay civil rights are a necessary precondition for the proper functioning of this system.

First, civil rights legislation for gay men and lesbians is warranted as being necessary for gays having equitable access to civic rights. By "civic rights," I mean rights to the impartial administration of civil and criminal law in defense of property and person. In the absence of such rights, there is no rule of law. An invisible minority historically subjected to widespread social discrimination has reasonably guaranteed access to these rights only when the minority is guaranteed nondiscrimination in employment, housing, and public services.

All would agree that civic rights are rights which everyone is supposed to have. All individuals must be assured the right to demand from government access to judicial procedures. But imagine the following scenario. Steve, who teaches math at a private suburban high school and coaches the swim team, on a weekend night heads to a popular gay bar. There he meets Tom, a self-employed contractor and father of two boys whose mother does not want Tom to have visitation rights, but is ignorant of his new life. Tom and Steve decide to walk to Tom's nearby flat, which he rents from a bigot who bemoans the fact that the community is going gay and refuses to rent to people he supposes to be gay; Tom's weekend visitations from his sons are his cover.

Meanwhile, at a nearby youth home for orphaned teenagers, the leader of one gang is taunting Tony, the leader of another gang, with the accusation of being a faggot. After much protestation, Tony claims he will prove once and for all that he is not a faggot, and hits the streets with his gang members, who tote with them the blunt and not so blunt instruments of the queerbasher's trade. Like a hyena pack upon a wildebeest, they descend on Tom and Steve, downing their victims in a blizzard of strokes and blows. Local residents coming home from parties and others walking their dogs witness the whole event.

Imagine that two miracles occur. One, a squad car happens by, and two, the police actually do their job. Tony and another of the fleeing queerbashers are caught and arrested on the felony charges of aggravated assault and attempted murder. Other squad cars arrive, and while witnesses' reports are gathered, Steve and Tom are taken to the nearest emergency room. Once Steve and Tom are in wards, the police arrive to take statements of complaint from them in what appears to be an open and shut case. But Steve knows the exposure of his sexual orientation in a trial will terminate his employment. And Tom knows the exposure of a trial would give his ex-wife the legal excuse she desires to deny his visitation rights. And he knows he will eventually lose his apartment. So neither man can reasonably risk pressing charges. Tony is released, and within twelve hours of attempting murder, he returns to the youth home hailed by all as a conquering hero. Rights for gays are a necessary condition for judicial access.

Any reader of gay urban tabloids knows that the events sketched here—miracles excepted—are typical daily occurrences. Every day, lesbians and gay men are in effect blackmailed by our judicial system. Our judicial system's threat of exposure prevents gay access to judicial protections. The example given above of latter-day lynch law falls within the sphere of criminal justice. Even more obviously, the same judicial blackmail occurs in civil cases.

It is unreasonable to expect anyone to give up that by which she lives, her employment, her shelter, her access to goods and services and to loved ones in order for judicial procedures to be carried out equitably, in order to demand legal protections.

Now what is bitterly paradoxical about this blackmail by the judiciary is that in the absence of civil rights legislation, it is a necessary consequence of two major virtues of the fair administration of justice with its determinations of guilt and innocence being based on a full examination of the facts. The first virtue is that trials are open to scrutiny by public and press. The second is that defendants must be able to be confronted by the witnesses against them and have compulsory process for obtaining witnesses in their favor, while conversely prosecutors must have the tools with which to press cases on behalf of victims. The result of these two virtues is that trials cast the private into the public realm.

That trials cast the private into the public realm puts the lie to those who claim that what gays do in private is no one else's business and should not be anyone else's business, so that on the one hand, gays do not need rights and on the other hand, they do not deserve rights, lest they make themselves public. If the judiciary system is to be open and fair, it is necessary that gays be granted civil rights. Otherwise judicial access becomes a right only for the dominant culture.

Widespread social prejudice against lesbians and gay men also has the effect of eclipsing their political rights. In the absence of gay civil rights legislation, gays are—over the range of issues which most centrally affect their minority status—effectively denied access to the political rights of the

First Amendment, that is, freedom of speech, freedom of press, freedom of assembly, and freedom to petition for the redress of grievances. In addition, they are especially denied the emergent constitutional right of association—an amalgam of the freedoms of speech and assembly—which establishes the right to join and be identified with other persons for common political goals.

Put concretely, does a gay person who has to laugh at and manufacture fag jokes in the workplace in order to deflect suspicion in an office which routinely fires gay employees have freedom to express his or her views on gay issues? Is it likely that such a person could reasonably risk appearing in public at a gay rights rally? Would such a person be able to participate in a march celebrating the Stonewall Riots and the start of gay activism? Would such a person be able to sign, let alone circulate, a petition protesting the firing of a gay worker? Would such a person likely try to persuade workmates to vote for a gay-positive city councilman? Would such a person sign a letter to the editor protesting abusive reportage of gay issues and events, or advocating the discussion of gay issues in schools? The answer to all these questions is "obviously not!" Such a person is usually so transfixed by fear that it is highly unlikely that he or she could even be persuaded to write out a check to a gay rights organization.

Further, it is hardly fair for gays as a statistical minority to be additionally encumbered in politics by having the majority of its members absent through social coercion from the public workings of the political process.

If First Amendment rights are not to be demoted to privileges to which only the dominant culture has access, then invisible minorities that are subject to widespread social discrimination will have to be guaranteed protection from those forces which maintain them in their position of invisibility. Civil rights protections take a very long step in that direction.

For at a minimum, all potentially effective political activity requires widely and pointedly disseminated political ideas. Only then is it possible for a minority political position on social policy to have a chance of becoming the majority opinion and so of becoming government policy and law. If the majority of people never have the occasion to change their opinions to those of a minority position, political rights would be pointless. Not surprisingly, then, all the actions protected by the First Amendment are public actions—speaking, publishing, petitioning, assembling, associating.

Now, a person who is a member of an invisible minority and who must remain invisible, hidden, and secreted in respect to her minority status as a condition for maintaining a livelihood is not free to be public about her minority status nor to incur suspicion by publicly associating with others who are open about their similar status. And so she is effectively denied all political power—except the right to vote. But voting aside, she will be denied the freedom to express her views in a public forum and to unite with or organize other like-minded individuals in an attempt to compete for votes which would elect persons who will support the policies advocated by her group. She is denied all effective use of legally available means of influencing public opinion prior to voting and all effective means of lobbying after elections are held.

It would seem incumbent upon government, then, to work toward ending those social conditions and mechanisms by which majority opinion maintains itself simply by the elimination of the hearing of possible alternative policies. To this end, government must prohibit nongovernmental agents from interfering with the political activities of individuals and groups. Thus, for instance, not only are political rallies constitutionally immune from government interference but also government is positively obliged to prohibit goon squads and hecklers from disrupting political rallies. Analogously, bigoted employers, landlords, and the like are the subtle goon squads and hecklers who deny gay men and lesbians access to political rights.

Up to the AIDS crisis, the meager energies and monies of the gay rights movement were directed almost exclusively at trying to get civil rights protections for lesbians and gay men. Without these legislated rights, which begin to bring gays into the procedures of democracy, gays have not been able to act very effectively on the issues about which gays reasonably would want to exert influence in democratic policy making, issues, for instance, concerning sex and solicitation law, licensing, zoning, judicial and prison reform, military and police policy, tax law, educational, medical and aging policy, affirmative action, law governing living associations and the transfer of property, and family law. By being effectively denied the public procedures of democracy, gays are incapable of defending their own interests on substantial issues of vital concern.

These various arguments should have a compelling cumulative force. Still, some people argue that there are legitimate reasons for exempting lesbians and gay men from some specific applications of general civil rights protections. Indeed the Civil Rights Act itself reasonably enough allows exemptions for discrimination against an otherwise protected category when the discrimination represents a "bona fide occupational qualification" reasonably necessary to the normal operation of a particular business or enterprise. For example, church-related hiring decisions may make religiously based discriminations. Are there some discriminations against gays which constitute such morally allowable discriminations in good faith? Not as a general matter.

Though the criteria for good faith discrimination are somewhat murky, the following general principle governing the establishment of good faith discriminations can be gleaned from our culture's moral experience. The principle is that simply citing the current existence of prejudice, bigotry, or discrimination in a society against some group or citing the obvious consequences of such prejudice, bigotry, or discrimination can never constitute a good reason in trying to establish a good faith discrimination against that group. The principle means that stigmas which are socially induced may not play a part in rational moral deliberations, that rationales for discrimination cannot be bootstrapped off of amassed private biases. For instance, a community could not legitimately claim that a by-law banning blacks from buying houses in the community was a good faith discrimination on the ground that whenever blacks move into a previously all-white area, property values plummet. This rationale is illegitimate, since current bigotry and its consequences are the only causes of the property values dropping—the result of white flight and the subsequent reduction in the size of the purchasing market.

In general, the fact that people discriminate can never be

cited as a good reason for institutionalizing discrimination. But even more clearly, the current existence of discrimination cannot ethically ground the continuance of the discrimination in the face of a moral presumption against discrimination. To hold otherwise is to admit the validity of the heckler's veto: to hold that it is acceptable for the state to prevent a speaker from speaking when a heckler in advance threatens disruption if the speaker does speak.

If this principle is accepted, it has a direct bearing on almost every case where people have tried to justify discrimination against gays as discrimination in good faith. An anti-gay prison ruling offers an especially pure example of the successful invocation of the heckler's veto. In 1984, the federal courts permitted the barring of the national gay Metropolitan Community Church from holding religious services in prisons although all other churches are allowed to hold services there. The courts bought without examination the government's contention that permitting the gay church's worship services was unacceptable because it would increase opportunities for identifying homosexual inmates and so expose these innocent churchgoing inmates to violent and predatory prisoners who would rape, intimidate, extort, and abuse them.

The reach of the principle is much wider. For one of its obvious ranges of application is cases where some joint project is a necessary part of a job. It is in this category of cases that good faith discriminations against gays are most often attempted.

Bans against gays in the armed forces and on police forces provide classic cases of attempts to establish good faith discrimination. In the early 1980s, the Pentagon articulated six reasons for banning gays: "The presence of such members adversely affects the ability of the armed forces [1] to maintain discipline, good order and morale, [2] to foster mutual trust and confidence among servicemembers, [3] to insure the integrity of the system of rank and command, [4] to facilitate assignment and worldwide deployment of servicemembers who frequently must live and work under close conditions affording minimal privacy, [5] to recruit and retain members of the armed forces, [and 6] to maintain the public acceptability of military service."

What all these claims have negatively in common is that none of them is based on the ability of gay soldiers to fulfill the duties of their stations. More generally, none of the claims is based on gays *doing* anything at all. What the six reasons have positively in common is that their force relies exclusively on current widespread bigoted attitudes against gays. They appeal to the bigotry and consequent disruptiveness of nongay soldiers (reasons 1, 2, 3, 4, and 5), who apparently are made "up-tight" by the mere presence of gay soldiers and officers, and so claim that they cannot work effectively in necessary joint projects with gay soldiers. The reasons appeal to the anti-gay prejudices of our own society (reason 6), especially that segment of it which constitutes potential recruits (reason 5), and to the anti-gay prejudices of other societies (reason 4). No reasons other than currently existing widespread prejudice and bigotry of others are appealed to here in order to justify a discriminatory policy against gays. So all six reasons violate the principle of good faith. Indeed the military's rationales are remarkably reminiscent of the military's rationales for segregating troops by race until President Truman ended the policy by executive order in 1948.

Another argument in which bad faith parades as good faith is one which tries to justify discrimination against gay teachers. It runs as follows: though openly gay teachers do not cause their students to become gay, an openly gay teacher might (inadvertently or not) cause a closeted gay student to become openly gay; the life of an openly gay person is a life of misery and suffering; therefore, openly gay teachers must be fired, since they promote misery and suffering. It seems that the second premise—life of misery—if true in some way peculiar to gays, is so in the main as the result of currently existing bigotry and discrimination in society of the very sort which the argument tries to enshrine into school board policy. So this argument too violates the principle of good faith.

Take as a final example of bad faith discrimination the arguments typically used in lesbian child-custody cases. Despite the near universal adoption of a gender-neutral "best interest of the child" test for determining which parent gets custody of a child, actual legal practice in nearly all jurisdictions still operates on a strong presumption in favor of giving custody to the mother *unless* the mother is a lesbian, in which case the presumption of parental fitness shifts sharply in the direction of the father. Sometimes the argument for this sharp shift is merely a statement of bigotry and stereotype. It runs: lesbians are immoral; lesbians cause their children to be lesbians; and therefore, lesbians cause their children to be immoral. When the shift is attempted to be justified as a good faith discrimination, the argument runs as follows: there is nothing inherently evil about a mother or child being lesbian, but nevertheless, since, while the child is growing, there will be strong social recrimination from peers and other parents against the child as it becomes known in the community that the mother is a lesbian, only by discriminating against lesbian mothers are their children spared unnecessary suffering. Here again bad faith is masquerading as good. Current bigotry and its consequences are cited as the only reason for perpetrating and institutionalizing discrimination. No one would seriously suggest that a fat mother should lose custody of her child because the child's friends might well tease the child about her mother's size. Clearly the "argument" is a mask of prejudice.

In 1984, the Supreme Court unanimously rejected the claim that recriminations which come to a child because her mother marries someone of another race can be legitimately taken into account in custody cases. The Court held, "The question . . . is whether the reality of private biases and the possible injury they might inflict are permissible considerations [in justifying discrimination]. We have little difficulty concluding that they are not. The Constitution cannot control . . . prejudices but neither can it tolerate them. Private biases may be outside the reach of the law, but the law cannot, directly or indirectly, give them effect." If this general principle were applied consistently in gay cases, discrimination against gays would come to an end.

Unfortunately, the passage of a lesbian and gay federal civil rights bill seems remote—even now when both houses of Congress and the White House are under the control of a political party which, at least on paper, is committed to such legislation. The gay movement's focus of the 1970s on civil rights shifted understandably in the 1980s to the AIDS crisis: one can't have rights if one's dead. Gay energies have been diverted from civil rights work to the crisis, which—prominently featured in anti-gay referendum initiatives—has prompted a backlash against such progress as gays did make in the 1970s. Getting civil rights for gays will depend upon correctly understanding government obligations and individual rights in the AIDS crisis.

CHAPTER 6

What to Do and Not to Do
about AIDS

In February 1993—a dozen years into the AIDS crisis—the research wing of the National Academy of Sciences released a study on the social impact of AIDS on America. It found that the disease had not fundamentally changed any basic social institution. However, the report ominously suggested that because the disease, both as scientifically appraised and as socially perceived, has remained largely confined to certain disfavored groups, society's response was shifting from generally liberal public health measures to punitive approaches which increasingly involve state coercion. Almost as a confirmation of the study's predictions, Congress in May 1993 reinstated a statutory ban on immigration by people with the virus which causes AIDS. Congress had originally imposed such a ban in 1987, but rescinded it in 1990. Further, if the report is right, the country's overall concern for the disease may well fade, and so too will diminish political pressures for government funding of AIDS research and patient care. Indeed, it appears that through the 1980s AIDS funding rose significantly only as AIDS came to be perceived as a threat to the dominant, nongay culture.

It is time to revisit arguments for and against government coercion and funding in the AIDS crisis.

In Cuba, the government has forced every citizen to be tested for the AIDS virus. Those testing positive are quarantined in internment camps, which the government euphemistically terms "a sanatorium system"—where, in the absence of a cure, the infected are locked up forever. The United States has not generally followed the Cuban model, though quarantines for people with the AIDS virus were set up in parts of the armed forces in 1985, existed at refugee detention centers from the late 1980s until 1993, and still exist in some prisons. Hysterical calls early in the crisis for quarantines went largely unheeded, as indeed they should have been, for reasons which show more generally that any specifically AIDS-directed coercive responses by the government are unwarranted.

The hysteria, when not simply an expression of old anti-gay prejudices, was based on the presumption that the disease is spread indiscriminately. This misperception and fear of general contagion was fixed in the public mind by *Life* magazine. In three-inch red letters, its July 1985 cover screamed to the nation "NOW NO ONE IS SAFE FROM AIDS." The magazine used as its allegedly compelling example a seemingly typical Pennsylvania family all but one of whose members has the disease. But the ways they became infected were all clear and discrete. The father was a hemophiliac infected before blood supplies were screened for the virus; his wife was infected through sex with him; and in the birthing process she conveyed the virus to a child. No one got the disease either mysteriously or through casual contact. The family example in fact was evidence *against* the article's generic contagion thesis. But into the 1990s, even some medically trained minds, like New York City Commissioner of Health Stephen C. Joseph, have tried to justify quarantines of people with the AIDS virus by miscomparing AIDS to such air- and water-borne diseases as typhus, influenza, contagious tuberculosis, and, for that matter, the common cold, all of which can be contracted simply from sharing public spaces with strangers.

For public policy purposes the most important fact about AIDS is not that it is deadly but that it, like hepatitis B, is caused by a blood-transmitted virus. AIDS is infectious, but not casually contagious. For the disease to spread, bodily fluids of someone with the virus must directly enter the bloodstream of another. And among bodily fluids, only blood, semen, vaginal fluids, and (possibly) breast milk have been implicated in the virus's transmission.

That the virus is blood transmitted means first and foremost that, with very rare exceptions, you get the virus from the actions you perform in conjunction with someone who already has the virus. Now that blood supplies are screened with a test for antibodies to the AIDS virus, the exceptions consist pretty much just of infants who are infected in being born. And no one has seriously suggested exerting the coercive power of government against mothers who infect their infants in this way, even when the mothers could be considered morally culpable.

The disease's mode of infection means that those infected are those whose actions directly contribute to their risk of infection—chiefly through sexual contact and shared hypodermic needles. The case for general, casual contagion cannot be made. In consequence, coercive government policy which is based on that fear is unwarranted. The extraordinary measures—including the suspension of civil liberties—which government might justifiably take, as in war, to prevent wholesale slaughter simply do not apply here. In particular, quarantining people with the AIDS virus in order to protect society at large from indiscriminate harm is unwarranted, as is the screening and exclusion of foreigners with the virus.

In addition, the mode of the transmission of AIDS means that other recent and increasingly prevalent attempts to institute mandatory testing and even to invoke criminal law to prevent the spread of AIDS are seriously misguided. Calls for various forms of mandatory testing have swept the nation in waves.

In 1987, a scattered rash of states passed laws making AIDS testing a requirement for getting a marriage license. Within two years, these laws had all been revoked. Couples in droves were simply driving to neighboring states to get married. When Illinois revoked its law, it also dropped all mandatory premarital testing for other venereal diseases. But reason was restored to AIDS policy only briefly.

The early 1990s saw a tidal wave of calls, including eighty-one votes in the U.S. Senate, for mandatory testing of all medical personnel who perform invasive procedures—mainly doctors and dentists. The calls were prompted by a Florida dentist who, apparently by failing to use even minimal sanitary procedures, infected six of his patients. In over a decade of medical invasions by infected personnel, these six cases are the only such infections to come to light. Here testing, with its enormous costs to the medical industry in terms of dollars and lost personnel, would prevent at best only the oddest of cases. Such mandatory testing is as rational as requiring people to stay indoors in order to reduce their risk of being hit by stray meteors. A far more rational approach, given the disease's mode of transmission, would be to promote and enforce medical hygiene, which would protect patients against a vast array of infections, not just AIDS.

Coercive sexual contact tracing is required in a few jurisdictions and permitted in many more. Where it is permitted but not required, public health agencies in fact do not do it. For they recognize that the labor-intensive practice is an inefficient means of stopping the disease, especially since it is one for which there is no current cure. And such tracing violates to boot the privacy rights which cover both sexual behavior and doctor-patient confidentiality. Public health agencies generally agree that safe-sex education is a more efficient use of scarce public health resources.

The latest trend to deploy the coercive, even punitive, power of government is to classify the knowing exposure of someone to the virus (say, through sexual behavior) as attempted murder or manslaughter. Half of the states have already adopted such laws. These laws argue that someone who exposes another to the virus is like a drunk driver or like someone shooting randomly in a theater. But the element of self-exposure in AIDS infections makes the disease's mode of transmission relevantly dissimilar to both of these fatal behaviors. Acts of will on the part of a bystander hit by a drunkenly driven car or the theatergoer struck by a bullet are not directed toward, do not actively participate in, nor contribute to the course of events that harms these people. Their presence by the road or in the theater is *merely* a necessary condition for the harm—as are millions of other states of affairs, such as their being born in the first place. One would not say that it was in virtue of their actions that they were harmed. But one would say this of the person who gets AIDS through sexual contacts or shared needles knowing that the virus can be transmitted this way. He actively participated in the very action that harms him. His deeds are not merely necessary conditions for harm but contribute to the causal chain by which he is harmed. It was in virtue of his actions that harm came to him. Unless he has been lied to, he is not a victim. In any case his sex partner is not a murderer. People, like valuable antiques, come as is. We would not want it any other way.

The coercive power of the state has also been used in many jurisdictions to close gay bathhouses. Most frequently the argument for these closures is a misguided analogy holding that the closures are no different from quarantining Typhoid Mary and removing the handle from her water pump, which if used will indiscriminately kill people since typhus is a water-borne disease. This argument fails for the same reason that calls for quarantines fail. More subtle arguments are paternalistic: closing bathhouses takes care of those who fail to take care of themselves, just as a parent coercively prevents a child from putting himself in harm's way. But these arguments too must fail. For if independence—the permission to guide one's life by one's own lights to an extent compatible with a like ability on the part of others—is, as it is, a major value, one cannot respect that value while preventing people from putting themselves at risk through voluntary associations. Voluntary associations are necessarily examples of people acting in accordance with the principle of independence, for mutual consent guarantees that the "compatible extent" proviso of the independence principle is fulfilled. But the state and even the courts have not been very sensitive to the distinction between one harming oneself and one harming another—nor has the medical establishment. It appears to all of them that a harm is a harm, a disease a disease, however caused or described. The moral difference, however, is enormous. Preventing a person from harming another is required by the principle of independence, but preventing someone from harming himself is incompatible with it. While no further justification is needed for the state to protect a person from others, a rather powerful justification is needed if the state is to be warranted in protecting a person from himself.

Occasionally, to be sure, the case for paternalism can be made to work. One legitimate way to justify paternalistic coercion is to claim as warrant for it a lack of rationality on the part of an agent (say, an insane person). By "rationality" here, I mean having relevant information and certain mental capacities, including the ability to reason from ends to means, but I do not presume that making the best possible assessment of means to an end is a requirement for rationality—error is compatible with rationality.

A presumption of an agent's rationality is a necessary condition for the very respect which is owed to her making her own decisions and guiding her life by them. Thus, paternalistic interference is warranted when a person is operating at risks which she is unable to assess due to diminished mental skills or lack of information. But education, not coercion, is the solution which is tailored to, and so appropriate for, such incapacities.

Far from justifying major paternalistic coercion of gay institutions, say, closing gay bathhouses, the argument from rationality here indeed suggests that paternalistic arguments surrounding AIDS are not even being advanced in good faith. For though education is one of government's highest spending priorities, governments have made no serious attempt to educate people about medically informed risks of AIDS and of safe alternatives to high-risk sexual practices. For example, school superintendents who have tried to introduce safe-sex education into curriculums have found themselves fired by their school boards. The latter, it can safely be assumed, agree with James Mason, who as the director of the Centers for Disease Control, claimed: "We don't think that citizens care to be funding material that encourages gay sex lifestyles." Thus any argument for governmental coercion of gay institutions on paternalistic grounds is probably disingenuous. At most the argument from rationality warrants placing warning labels on bathhouses as they are placed on cigarettes, the use of which also threatens death.

The other legitimate argument for paternalistic coercion is that one should be protected from ceding away the very conditions that enable one to be an independent agent. Thus one cannot legitimately contract to become a slave or sign away rights to the equitable administration of justice. Is exposing oneself to AIDS relevantly like contracting into slavery?

No, first, slavery by definition is a condition of lost independence. However, as with other venereal diseases, not every sexual encounter—even a maximally "unsafe" one—with an infected partner causes a person to become infected. Studies of couples with one infected partner have shown that susceptibility varies widely from person to person. And it is known from hepatitis B studies that even when no precautions are taken against the transmission of blood-borne diseases, they only ever partially saturate a population which exposes itself to them—that is, the percent of infected members among those potentially infected reaches a certain point and goes no higher. With the hepatitis B virus, the plateau is about 66 percent; with the much harder to contract AIDS virus, the percent is lower. Because the risks are high but the results not invariably catastrophic, putting oneself at risk for AIDS becomes less like contracting into slavery and more like being a racecar driver, mountain climber, logger, or astronaut. In the absence of inevitability, the assessment of risk should be left to the individual, and indeed, as the examples of space flight, mountaineering, logging, and racecar driving show, this is the considered standard of society.

Second, sex is one of the central values of human life. Individuals, not government, must make the difficult choices where values centrally affecting the self come into conflict. That such choice falls to the individual is generally recognized where religious ideals and health are the conflicting values. The state cannot legitimately make the trade-offs that an informed adult will make between religious values and health by, say, coercing an adult—for the sake of preserving his own independence—to have a blood transfusion against his Christian Scientist belief that a transfusion, even a coerced one, will damn him for all eternity. So, sexual attitudes and acts in accord with them are not fit subjects of state coercion for the individual's own good, even when that good is the continued ability to make choices.

The centrality of sex to individual lives, however, provides a justification for state funding for preventive AIDS research. People ought not to be in the position where they have to make trade-offs between the components of a complete life. Ending the conflict of central personal values will be especially attractive when the means to it place no nearly comparable burden on others. The case at hand requires tax dollars for basic immunological research and applied viral research. Yet, given the ends likely to be achieved and assuming an equitable tax system, taxation places no comparable burden on those taxed.

A second argument for preventive AIDS funding is that no one should have to live in a condition of terror. Imagine a prisoner who is never actually tortured but who daily witnesses the torture of others. His witnessings are not merely one more unpleasant component of prison life, on a par, say, with tasteless food. Rather, both the torture victims and the observer have experienced cruel and unusual punishment. Constantly expected but uncertain pain and destruction seizes up the mind, destroying the equanimity necessary for thinking, deciding, and acting, and grotesquely turns the mind against itself, punishing itself as a way to avoid uncertainty and to produce the appearance of order and progression. Human dignity on pretty much any account is here destroyed.

Gay men now live in such a condition of generalized terror. When there were few cases of AIDS and its horrors seemed personally remote, gay men understandably dealt with it as the mind can do with forebodings on the horizon—they avoided it through denial, a typical coping mechanism of the already beleaguered. But as the number of AIDS cases rose exponentially, spreading from cities to towns and leaving nearly everyone with the memory of lost acquaintances, the terror of constantly expected but uncertain destruction and its attendant contortions have become quite general. It turns out, for instance, that gay doctors, who cannot easily sustain the denial stage, experience more anxiety and mental disturbances over AIDS than people who actually have the disease. Everyone exposed to terror has a positive claim that it be ended.

Though AIDS is a disease caught in a condition where one has put oneself at risk, nevertheless gay men in general ought in consequence of certain natural and cultural forces to be viewed as morally innocent in its contagion and spread. The disease should not be viewed as a matter of paying the piper. And so even in the absence of justifications for perfectly general government health-care plans, funding should nevertheless be provided for the care of those whose life chances in civil society have been permanently destroyed by natural catastrophes that elude the protections of civil defense—so that in dying they might at least avoid unnecessary suffering and the indignity to which this disease in particular tends to expose patients.

The general case for innocence is one to be made from an accumulation of factors. Consider, first, that the incubation period for the disease is indeterminately long. This means that there are people who even under maximal conditions of risk avoidance—totally swearing off sex on first hearing in 1981 of the disease as potentially contagious—are still even now coming down with the disease. Social policy has no way of telling who these innocent people are. Second, educational material that would make people aware of their risks has not been made available, indeed in many cases has been blocked, by governments. And the mass media continue to be more than a little reluctant to provide details of safe-sex practices.

No television network will air ads for condoms. Public service announcements on AIDS tell the audience to be concerned about AIDS, but give no safe-sex information. So many people even now are taking risks in situations of constrained information. These people too should be viewed as innocent.

Yet, even in conditions of complete information, most individuals are not very good at risk management. So even with a knowledge of the likelihood of contagion per sexual contact, many people would still make mistakes. Such errors, however, are not the product of negligence: it's just that most human beings have very poor intuitions about statistics and probabilities. That such intuitions are so poor makes a big difference in assigning fault to individuals. Successful choice and guilt do not jointly exhaust the moral field. The high value society places on choice despite a significant propensity of people to make poor choices creates a zone of the failed innocent.

Further, there are a number of reasons why the gay sexual agent, even with complete knowledge and clear capacities, might be led to take risks which many would think extraordinary. First, sex drive is not something over which one has an unrestrained control. The Centers for Disease Control now recommend that gay men simply be celibate—unless they have lived in completely monogamous, long-term relationships. This advice seems remote from reality and quite oblivious to the cussedness of sex and culture. On the one hand, the recurring and intrusive nature of sexual desire guarantees that in general gay men, like others, will not be celibate. On the other, long-term gay relations, if not as rare as adamant, are at least as rare as rubies. And in any case fear is a particularly poor forge for working the most delicate of human bonds with a view to future domestic continence.

Worse still for the likely escape from risk is the layering over of sexual drive with certain cultural forces. Even now most men who have gay sex are not gay self-identified and, in order to keep jobs, preserve marriages, and otherwise accommodate the dominant culture as a condition for social life, they necessarily have sex on the run. Many of these men consciously do not have safe-sex, lest that, paired with the dominant culture's virtual identification of AIDS and "queers," force them to a recognition that they themselves are after all "queer."

Society, in focusing its concerns exclusively on the single characteristic by which an individual deviates from the norm, makes that one characteristic into the whole person: the homosexual, the faggot. Forthright gays in the process of reappropriating for themselves that very characteristic by which the dominant culture transfixes them, indeed reinforce (reasonably enough) its very centrality to themselves. As a result, something more than just pleasure and the fulfillment of need is wrapped up in sex for gays. With some slight exceptions like the gay choral movement, gay political organizations, and (sure enough) AIDS support groups, sex is the only mode in which gays in current culture are allowed to identify themselves to themselves. Self-respect, such as it is, for gay men in our culture is often the product of a robust sex life.

Even so, it is likely that the core of that respect is poisoned. One cannot completely withdraw oneself from one's culture, in this case a culture that takes gays to be worth less than nongays and very likely to be entirely worthless. In this circumstance, one is likely to make unwise decisions about one's sex life. Self-hatred and sexual desire tend to become fused. Just as violence—even against oneself (as in the "rough trade" phenomenon)—can be an especially effective object of sexual arousal, so can death—even one's own. AIDS is such a situation into which many gay men are drifting in part as the fulfillment of the dominant culture's appraisal of them, in part as a spin-off from the search for self-respect in a society that thwarts it. This is not idle speculation: it turns out that the same gay doctors who have extreme anxieties over the AIDS crisis have proven to be particularly unable to live by the safe-sex guidelines they prescribe to others. And in a similar pattern, one reminiscent of other survivor syndromes, it also turns out that partners who suffer through the AIDS death of their lovers frequently themselves then go on binges of unsafe sex.

Doctors cure, but there is no cure. Rather, care for AIDS patients chiefly requires routine nursing and hospice care. The disease is typically characterized by a progressive loss of energy and bodily control, punctuated by opportunistic infections which bring with them debilitating pain, disorientation, incontinence, and an inability to perform even basic functions without assistance. Historically, routine nursing and hospice functions have been performed by family members, and long-term terminal illnesses were thus not major public policy concerns.

Compensatory justice requires that hospice and nursing care is owed to gay patients by the state in consequence of society's and government's prohibition against the creation of gay families. If society barred a motorcyclist from wearing a helmet which he would have worn, he would certainly be

owed compensation from society for any injury which a helmet could have prevented. So too, in forbidding gay families,
society owes gays the protections and comforts which it
prevents them from acquiring on their own. It perhaps goes
without saying that attempts of gays to create blood relations
and extended families of their own have been severely bur-
dened by both society and the state. At every turn, gays have
been unfairly hampered in creating their own nurturing families.

Compassion would suggest, and compensatory justice
should require, that the day-to-day care of the final-stage
AIDS patient be provided in lieu of the care he would have
likely had but for society's hindering his creation of his own
family.

CHAPTER 7

Understanding Gays in the Military

Fundamentalists may be right: events turn markedly for the worse immediately before the emergence of the messianic era. At least this seems to be the case for gays in the military.

After a fifty-year policy that excluded from military service anyone the service considered to be homosexual, the nation in 1993 adopted a more complicated policy: the military is barred from asking its members which of them are gay, but is required to discharge any member who says he or she is gay. The policy, popularly dubbed "Don't Ask, Don't Tell," is not one which can be morally acceptable to gays, or indeed to anyone who has respect for human beings.

The past policy of rooting out and totally excluding gay men and lesbians at least had the virtue of appearing to treat gays as devils—evil forces set on destruction and corruption. As we know from Dante and Milton, devils can be charming, vibrant, intriguing fellows. Devils are even creatures worthy of respect for who they are, though not for what they do. After all, they are at heart angels—angels who have gone wrong and do wrong. And devils, remember, are creatures about whom we can talk, indeed should talk, so we can find them out.

The moral dynamics of "Don't Ask, Don't Tell" treat gays differently and worse. In this policy, gays are not demonized as agents to be feared for what they might do, but rather are viewed as the horrible, the disgusting, the loathsome, the unspeakably gross—in short, as abject beings. Core cases of abject beings are excrement, vomit, pus, and the smells associated with these. Such repulsive matters are expelled from the body's insides in its very process of living, but tend to cling to it, and so are always in need of being cleansed away. Even to name these matters is thought to be disgusting, since the names, like scents, bring the matters back again to consciousness.

It is just exactly around these (only ever half-acknowledged) abject matters that society sets up rituals of the form Don't Ask, Don't Tell. Take, for example, the case of flatulence in a crowded elevator: no one tells; no one asks; everyone acts as though nothing is amiss, and so reinforces the abject thing's status as loathsome. When faced or confronted with the abject, people have visceral responses of aversion, distraction, vertigo, even nausea, and so, to the extent possible, people systematically act as if the abject does not exist, even though they secretly and deeply know it does.

This daunting effort to repress knowing and acknowledgment requires a blanket of silence to be cast over the abject thing. In order to be systematic, the silence must be ritualized. To tell of the abject is to break a taboo. To ask of the abject is to be reminded of its constantly recurring, lurking, louring presence just beyond oneself.

In essence, the Pentagon order Don't Ask, Don't Tell ritualizes into a national paradigm The Closet—with its open secret and commitment to the abject standing and worthlessness of gays. The order says that as long as *you* gays act as though *we* people don't know who you are, we will act as though you don't exist, and thus in our willing ignorance, recommit ourselves to viewing your status as loathsome and repulsive.

The chief problem of the social institution of the closet is not that it promotes hypocrisy, requires lies, sets snares, blames the victim when snared, and causes unhappiness—though it does have all these results. No, the chief problem with the closet is that it treats gays as less than human, less than animal, less even than vegetable—it treats gays as reeking scum, the breath of death.

Each time a gay person finds the closet morally acceptable to himself or others, he degrades himself as gay and sinks to the level of abjection dictated for gays by the dominant culture. No gay person with sufficient self-respect and dignity can require that another gay person be viewed in this way. And no one at all can accept the Don't Ask, Don't Tell policy and suppose that at the same time he or she is treating gays as people.

Still, it seems that long-range the policy will prove unworkable in practice. The Pentagon's detailed directives institutionalizing the policy are a rat's nest of confused and contradictory impulses. More generally, the Pentagon will likely learn that "don't ask" and "don't tell" do not together guarantee "don't know." Even the collusion of gay soldier and investigative board is not sufficient to assure ignorance and denial. On the one hand, it is practically impossible for a soldier to erase every indicator of his or her desire; the military closet is always giving its secret away no matter what its occupant does. On the other hand, if a straight soldier or a gay civilian "outs" a gay soldier, then again the delicately poised architecture of ritual and taboo collapses.

The instability of the policy will likely lead either to a reinstatement of the old total ban, or more likely to a complete lifting of the ban on gays and gay presence in the military. If the latter occurs, the nation as a whole will be the chief gainer. The ban on gays in the military goes to the heart of the nation's understanding of what it means to be a person. Lifting the ban will transform the nation for the better, since what counts as citizenship itself will be improved.

The military is nominally intended to *defend* what the country is, but as its racial and gender histories show, it is the chief institution by which the nation *defines* what the country is and what is to count as full personhood and full citizenship. Take the Civil War. Even though the North was fighting (at least in part) to end black slavery, both North and South initially conceived the war as one to be carried out only between white men—full citizens. President Lincoln (it may come as a surprise to learn) was not seeking full citizenship for blacks, did not entertain black equal protection, and opposed the black vote. He thought blacks should be like white women as far as citizenship was concerned. But under the press of necessity, both sides, by the war's end, had resorted to the deployment of black combat troops. For many southerners, this reconfiguration of the army was the equivalent of having lost the war even before hostilities' end. For in being combatants, blacks had changed their definition and assumed the rank of full citizens. They could no longer be thought of as slaves. The North cast this conceptual shift into institutional, indeed constitutional form. The Fourteenth Amendment granted full citizenship and equal protection rights to blacks, and the Fifteenth Amendment conferred the vote on black men. At least on the plane of the nation's *ideals,* the Civil War and its Amendments catapulted the nation far ahead of Lincoln's understanding of race.

The ban on homosexual presence in the military operates at a similar profound level of national definition. Straight soldiers' skittishness, which the military uses to try to justify the suppression of gays, is a mere surface phenomenon masking a much deeper and wider cultural anxiety about gay men—anxiety over understanding the male body as a penetrable object. For the military, the real person, the full citizen, is defined as one who must penetrate while never being penetrated. Conversely, it defines the enemy as a potentially penetrating but actually penetrated body. The citizen warrior first "penetrates" the enemy's lines and then penetrates the enemy himself for the kill.

But with the development of military tactics and technologies in the opening decades of this century, the notions of what is penetrated and what counts as penetration became fuzzy in practice. Battle lines became vague. And those sturdy penetrators—sword, lance, and bayonet—gave way to strafing, remote bombing, and radiation as what kills. The resulting ambiguity in military practice called for a refocusing and resolidification of the distinction between the penetrable and the impenetrable at the level of the military's conception of itself. And so with the coming of the Second World War, general exclusions from the military for immorality crystallized in 1942 into an explicit ban on homosexuals.

The categories of heterosexual and homosexual definition provide both the cultural symbols for and social undergirding to our contemporary understanding of battle and citizenship. To allow gay men—willingly penetrable penetrators—to go into battle would be (so it goes) to confuse warriors with the enemy, full citizens with those worthy of death, to confuse conquest and defeat, glory and damnation. Lest this claim seem too grand, it is the very scenario that General Norman Schwarzkopf, commander of the U.S. forces in the 1991 Persian Gulf War, painted in May 1993 before the Senate Armed Services Committee. The media treated his testimony as the final undoing of efforts to lift the ban on gays in the military. He claimed that open gays in the military would make U.S. soldiers "just like many of the Iraqi troops who sat in the deserts of Kuwait," demoralized, hapless, essentially passive as allied troops rolled through, defeating them, the fourth largest army in the world, in a matter of days. Such is the fearsome power of gay presence.

The same cultural configuration subsidiarily explains the traditional defining of women out of combat roles, roles that call for shooting guns. In the modern army, it is socially acceptable for women to be killed in battle—while, for instance, laying communication wire across the battle front or flying troop transport planes through battle zones. So, paternalistic arguments tendered to explain the barring of women from combat roles simply do not track reality. Rather if women—culturally viewed essentially as penetrable bodies—were to be killers, combatants, and so conceptualized not as penetrable bodies but as penetrators, that again would challenge the definition of full citizens as impenetrable bodies and the enemy as penetrable bodies. The real reason, the deep reason, why women have traditionally been barred from combat and gay people (culturally read, gay men) have traditionally been barred from the military altogether is that the exclusions are essential machinery in the cultural project that defines full citizens as impenetrable penetrators.

If the nation eventually lifts its ban on gay soldiers, it will not simply be acknowledging finally the full status of gays as citizens in America—important as that recognition on its own is. It will also begin, as did the ending of slavery, to transform our understanding of who we are as people. It will change our ideals, whatever our failed or partial practices of them may be. The ending of slavery meant that a person may no longer view another essentially as just an instrument or tool in his or her own projects. The end of the military's ban on gay presence will extend this line of cultural thinking and point in the direction of equally momentous cultural change and moral improvement.

It will allow everyone to have a more relaxed view of human agency and experience the universe as a more hospitable, commodious, and, in turn, respect-worthy abode. The citizen need not define himself as conqueror, need not view the universe and others as something that must be subjugated to or killed by his intrusive presence in order to be good. One need not invade others to be what one is. One may be open to being, rather than stand in opposition to it. Reason can then include a healthy element of contemplation, rather than being limited to instrumental uses, calculations of utility, and the analysis of things into manageable parts. We will be less in need of grace, for we shall be more graceful. We will be less in need of divine intervention, for we will stand more receptive to each other. We can worry less about being ineffectual and weak. We will be more merciful to those who fail, for we will have less to prove in ourselves. A kinder, gentler nation will finally become a live possibility. We will be more self-contained and self-confident, even as we are more easily able to make connections with each other. We will be more productive when we view productivity as creation and care rather than as management and control. We will be more self-sufficient, as we release for individual flourishing the massive cultural energy now wasted in the anxiety required to prop up the false symbol of self-sufficiency—impenetrability.

Straight soldiers who are unable to follow along with society on this journey of transformation can always stoop rather than bend over for soap dropped in the shower.

ENVOI

America's Promise

How can individuals, families, and organizations begin to help America make good its promise of equal justice under law, to realize its belief that all people are created equal, and to confirm its allegiance to liberty and justice for all?

1. All Americans, whether you know it or not, someone in your life is gay. Acknowledge this fact, and so know too that how things turn out for gays makes a difference to someone you love.

2. When you hear anti-gay aspersions and jokes, draw up some moral courage and confront the speaker by naming them as bigotry. Anti-gay slang and jokes can work their insidious ends only with your complicity in evil.

3. Help keep open channels of communication and the flow of ideas on gay issues. Block renewed attempts to silence gay people and issues—whether among soldiers, in schools, behind legislative committee doors, or at art galleries. Silencing

is shame, ignorance, stultification, and a recommitment to the past.

Arguments are on the side of gays. Talk disseminates them. Gay life and experience are on the side of justice. Talk displays them. The tactics and targets of anti-gay forces tacitly acknowledge that their success depends upon keeping in place the old taboos against talking about gays, refurbishing and resolidifying them when necessary. Flood these efforts with truth.

4. Nongay people, begin seeking out joint projects with openly gay people. Studies have found that the best way to reduce prejudice—as has been done with race tensions in the military—is for different groups to work together on projects that do not directly address their differences. Such projects could easily be found in the work that needs to be done in the AIDS crisis.

Acknowledge that many perks, privileges, opportunities, benefits, and rights flow to you because of your status as straight and not because of either your personhood or your actions. This channeling of goods is not a matter of natural destiny but of social choice. Fairness will require that these social goods be distributed to everyone.

5. Members of families, repeat after me: "We should have acknowledged Uncle Jack was gay. That we didn't make the effort, didn't allow ourselves to know and show concern means that he was a ghost in our lives and we very likely were deadweight in his."

Parents, admit that some of your children will turn out to

be gay, and then decide how you want America's children to live and learn. Know that now one-third of teenage suicides are lesbian and gay youth, that one-third of all lesbian and gay youth attempt suicide, and that one-half of gay male teenagers who show up at urban public health clinics are infected with the virus that causes AIDS. Justice saves lives— maybe those of your kids.

6. Organizations, be aware of the consequences your activities have on gay values and experience. Business leaders, know that formal nondiscrimination clauses, important as they are, do little to erase the day-to-day indignities that beset your gay employees. Include gay issues in your diversity training programs. Tell government that your domestic partnership programs are working and should point the way to the legal acknowledgment of gay marriages. Labor unions, don't broadcast ads that romanticize groups like the Boy Scouts, who as a matter of policy discriminate against gays. Don't try to legitimize your cause as all-American in ways that make gays look un-American.

7. Churches, be aware of the real-world effects of your frequently asserted claim that you hate only the sin, not the sinner. Examine your hearts to see whether you really even believe it or whether the clever phrase isn't just a smiling mask for bigotry. Its real-world effects are to promote hatred and rationalize violence against gay people.

Be aware too that the rights which gay people seek are simply the same rights to freedom and equality which the Constitution and the Civil Rights Act afford to religious groups and which have made America such a fertile ground for religious experimentation, variety, and expression.

8. Straight women and other nongay minorities, know that while the causes of oppression may well differ from minority to minority, the structures of oppression and inequality are the same. So even though your fortunes and those of gays may not have been linked in the past, they are linked now as we all look to the future and to remedies in justice.

9. Straight men, while your dignity is not at stake in establishing justice for gays, your freedom is. As long as you define yourself in terms of some type and find your worth in putting down those of another type, then you will be trapped by the expectations and requirements of your type and you will always be subject to social blackmail for perceived failures to live up to type. If you use anti-gay attitudes and behaviors to prop up your perception of your gender, and hold your gender, rather than your accomplishments, as what defines you as good, then you will never be able just to be yourself, you will never realize the distinctive human potential for freedom—the ability to develop your own capacities in your own way.

10. Gay people, the landscape is littered with phony friends. Be wary of politicians and leaders, gay or not, who promise you happiness tomorrow if only you are just good enough today by the standards of those who have traditionally oppressed you. You can never be *that* good, for *they* judge you by what you are, not by what you do.

Change is in the air. But we cannot be sure that great reversals are not in store or even that the long arc of the universe does in the end bend toward justice.

Nevertheless, stay the course. For we can be sure that if we take dignity and the openness which that entails as our polestar and if we guide our lives by principle and certify them with the sacrifice which principled living entails, then to a significant degree, gay justice can be ours through our own actions, our worth shining forth unsullied, clear, and free.

ACKNOWLEDGMENTS

My thanks go to James Rachels for suggesting this project to me years back, to Claudia Mills and Arthur Evenchik for showing me initially how it might be done, and to the good folk at Beacon Press, especially my editor, Deborah Chasman, for shaping the project and coaxing it into reality.

I am also grateful to my librarian, John M. Littlewood, my friend, Simon D. Stern, and my husband, Robert W. Switzer.

The book was begun while I was a fellow in the University of Illinois Program for the Study of Cultural Values and Ethics. It was finished while I was an associate in the university's Center for Advanced Study. I applaud these sources for the opportunities they have afforded me.